THE
COMPLETE
IDIOT'S
GUIDE® TO

Global Economics

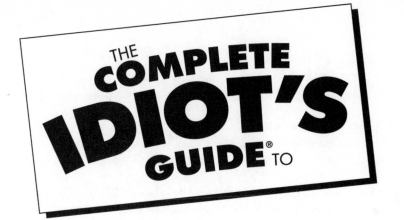

THE
COMPLETE
IDIOT'S
GUIDE® TO

Global
Economics

Craig Hovey with Gregory Rehmke

ALPHA

A member of Penguin Group (USA) Inc.

ALPHA BOOKS

Published by the Penguin Group

Penguin Group (USA) Inc., 375 Hudson Street, New York, New York 10014, U.S.A.

Penguin Group (Canada), 10 Alcorn Avenue, Toronto, Ontario, Canada M4V 3B2 (a division of Pearson Penguin Canada Inc.)

Penguin Books Ltd, 80 Strand, London WC2R 0RL, England

Penguin Ireland, 25 St Stephen's Green, Dublin 2, Ireland (a division of Penguin Books Ltd)

Penguin Group (Australia), 250 Camberwell Road, Camberwell, Victoria 3124, Australia (a division of Pearson Australia Group Pty Ltd)

Penguin Books India Pvt Ltd, 11 Community Centre, Panchsheel Park, New Delhi—110 017, India

Penguin Group (NZ), cnr Airborne and Rosedale Roads, Albany, Auckland 1310, New Zealand (a division of Pearson New Zealand Ltd)

Penguin Books (South Africa) (Pty) Ltd, 24 Sturdee Avenue, Rosebank, Johannesburg 2196, South Africa

Penguin Books Ltd, Registered Offices: 80 Strand, London WC2R 0RL, England

Copyright © 2008 by Craig Hovey

International Standard Book Number: 978-1-59257-660-9
Library of Congress Catalog Card Number: 2007935858

10 09 08   8 7 6 5 4 3 2 1

Interpretation of the printing code: The rightmost number of the first series of numbers is the year of the book's printing; the rightmost number of the second series of numbers is the number of the book's printing. For example, a printing code of 08-1 shows that the first printing occurred in 2008.

Printed in the United States of America

Most Alpha books are available at special quantity discounts for bulk purchases for sales promotions, premiums, fundraising, or educational use. Special books, or book excerpts, can also be created to fit specific needs.

For details, write: Special Markets, Alpha Books, 375 Hudson Street, New York, NY 10014.

Publisher: *Marie Butler-Knight*
Editorial Director: *Mike Sanders*
Managing Editor: *Billy Fields*
Editorial Director/Acquisitions Editor: *Paul Dinas*
Development Editor: *Julie Bess*
Copy Editor: *Tricia Liebig*

Cartoonist: *Richard King*
Cover Designer: *Bill Thomas*
Book Designer: *Trina Wurst*
Indexer: *Brad Herriman*
Layout: *Brian Massey and Chad Dressler*
Proofreader: *John Etchison*

Contents at a Glance

Contents

Introduction

Why are we hearing so much more about globalization and the economic issues that are a major component of it today than ever before? Between major advances in technology, dropping costs of communication and transport, and widespread innovation occurring at a pace never seen before, distance and national borders are no longer the barriers they used to be. In the past, most people rarely ventured outside their home country; today, the hands of foreigners can be seen in myriad goods and services we use every day.

Fears abound that foreigners are taking jobs and markets that used to be ours exclusively, with the result being that their standards of living will rise at the expense of ours. However, evidence is emerging that the economies most open to trade with others are the wealthiest, and those who try hardest to keep the rest of the world at bay end up impoverishing themselves. Especially when it comes to issues such as trade, what economics teaches is that the obvious and intuitive answers are often wrong. Fortunately, the right answers can be understood by applying a collection of tools that are not difficult to master.

Many among us worry that the trade deficit spells doom, but don't look at the other side of the equation, which shows how the money we spend on products made in other countries comes back to the United States in the form of investment, which is then used to create new businesses and jobs at home. To understand this relationship, all that is necessary is a basic familiarity with our system of national accounts, an easy thing to gain.

Another thing economics shows us is that competition is less important than the capacity to meet the needs and wants of other individuals and nations. You don't need to be the best at everything, or even anything—you just need to make contributions that others will give you something of value in exchange for. Go figure!

Assumptions, theories, and concepts are always open to varying interpretations. Although economics is considered a science in the sense that it is an organized method of inquiry, it is not a science in the sense that a particular experiment can be repeated over and over with the result being predictable. Human beings are not always predictable, and even when they are in a particular case, the fact that we can observe, learn, and change our minds means that our actions can change radically in the future. This means that there is plenty of room for disagreement in economics. *The Complete Idiot's Guide to Global Economics* isn't written to be taken as words inscribed in a tablet for all time, but as a presentation of a fascinating topic that allows readers to go forth and think for themselves.

The Road Ahead

Part 1, "Is the World Everybody's Oyster Now?," introduces you to global economics and provides an overview of basic economic principles.

Part 2, "Zero-Sum Games Are for Losers," looks at why global trade, rather than being a competition that mandates that winners win at the expense of losers, is a process that can enrich all nations involved.

Part 3, "Knock Down the Old Gray Walls," is a realistic examination of the kinds of things countries around the globe do to protect themselves from foreign competitors—while also trying to reap maximum benefits from the process themselves.

Part 4, "Show Us the Money," is devoted to how countries with different currencies are able to buy and sell goods and services from countries all across the world. Each country will see the value of their currency change, for better or worse, over time, and you learn the reasons why.

Part 5, "The Territories Less Explored," is where we get a chance to look at current issues of particular interest, such as global warming, terrorism, dumping, and quality-of-life issues. Economics provides us with a set of tools that can be used to examine almost any nook and cranny, and here you get to do just that.

Signposts You'll See

In the pages ahead, you'll come across some regular features designed to help you understand global economics and what it means for people living in the real world.

Did You Know? _____

Interesting and illustrative factual information on global economics and the countries who participate in the global economy (rates of economic growth, exports and imports, emerging industries, and so on) can be found here.

EconoTalk

Common terms, phrases, and concepts used in the study of global economics are simply and clearly defined.

Warning, Pothole Ahead!

Readers are warned of common mistakes in thinking and logic that often occur in the study of global economics.

Acknowledgments

It has been my privilege to teach and learn from many wonderful students during my career. In particular during the writing of this book were two cohorts in the Executive MBA Program at St. John Fisher College. Despite having full-time jobs and many a full-time family while they attended a full-time academic program that took up many a weeknight and wiped out a whole slew of Saturday mornings and afternoons, they (almost) always brought an enthusiasm and insight to our economics classes that raised the level and made the "dismal science" a fun thing to learn about.

I also thank Paul Dinas and everybody else at Alpha Books who do such a great job of producing this unique series of books and helped make mine worthy of being included.

Craig Hovey

Trademarks

All terms mentioned in this book that are known to be or are suspected of being trademarks or service marks have been appropriately capitalized. Alpha Books and Penguin Group (USA) Inc. cannot attest to the accuracy of this information. Use of a term in this book should not be regarded as affecting the validity of any trademark or service mark.

Part 1

Is the World Everybody's Oyster Now?

Over the last couple decades, more and more of the everyday goods that people wear, consume, and drive have been made in distant countries. And in those distant countries, more and more people watch American movies, use American software and consulting services, eat American hamburgers, and sip American lattés.

This part introduces you to global economics and provides an overview of the broad issues. The basics of economics are also reviewed to help you understand the material throughout these chapters.

"How much wool do you need, Mr. Yakasi?"

It's a Small World After All

In This Chapter

- Global economics is all around us
- The United States' participation in global economics
- Technology's part in the growth of global trade

What does it mean when we hear that economies are globalizing and that the world is becoming a "flatter" place? Simply that individuals, businesses, and countries around the world are trading more and more resources—including their own time—with each other in the quest to improve living standards and the quality of life.

You Can't Leave Home Without It

These days you can't even walk out the front door without the weight of the world on your shoulders, or on your head, hands, hips, feet, or in your pocket. That t-shirt may have started off as cotton grown in Texas, but that cotton was likely harvested and sent to China and made into a shirt in a factory outside Shanghai, and may have made a few more stops in other parts of the world before appearing in the mall where it was bought. Even after you are done with that t-shirt, its travels may not be over. If it is in good shape and you donate it to a charity, it could end up being sold secondhand from a wooden stall in Kenya. (You can learn more about the global journey of t-shirts in Pietra Rivoli's fascinating book, *Travels of a T-Shirt in the Global Economy*.) There are poor people here who shop at Goodwill, St. Vincent de Paul, and other thrift stores, but there are far more and far poorer people overseas. Few of the clothes given to charity in the United States stay within the country. Instead, they are sold to companies known as "ragpickers" who sort, fumigate, bale, and sell them abroad. Used clothing is one of the top American exports to sub-Saharan Africa.

Do you wear baseball caps? Sure, the logo comes from an American team, but the cap itself could have been made in Pakistan. What about your favorite pair of jeans? Surely they are strictly an American product, right—a legacy of cowboys and miners in the West of the nineteenth century? During the 1990s, in the face of stiff competition from overseas brands, the Levi Strauss Company closed most of its American and Canadian manufacturers of jeans and began producing the finished pants in factories located in countries such as Vietnam, Colombia, Mexico, and China. Levi Strauss himself was an import and came to California from Bavaria in 1853.

Did You Know? _____

Making, or protesting, the case for global trade is nothing new. Adam Smith, the "father of economics," laid out the case in favor of it in 1776 within his book *The Wealth of Nations*:

"It is the maxim of every prudent master of a family, never to attempt to make at home what it will cost him more to make than to buy … What is prudence in the conduct of every private family, can scarce be folly in that of a great kingdom. If a foreign country can supply us with a commodity cheaper than we ourselves can make it, better buy it of them with some part of the product of our own industry, employed in a way in which we have some advantage."

Running out the door in a pair of sneakers, you are again treading with a foreign-made good that could have been designed in Oregon but sewn in a factory in Indonesia or Thailand. On the way to your car, you make a call on a cell phone that was designed in South Korea or Finland with software from California and computer chips from Texas and Malaysia. The car itself has the name of a foreign-owned company on it, such as Toyota or Subaru. You might assume it was manufactured in Japan, but in this case there is an excellent chance it was assembled in the United

States—maybe even in a heartland state such as Indiana. Say you drive this car to an appointment with your physician and she examines you while wearing latex gloves. Though the natural rubber latex comes from the *Havea brazilienis* tree, which is native to South America, approximately 16 million acres is devoted to growing them in Asia, where 95 percent of the world's natural rubber supply is produced.

The point here is that no matter where you go or what you do, you participate in a sophisticated, far-flung global economy whose members coordinate production and trade goods and services across borders to a degree never seen before. And guess what? Globalization is ongoing, and economic interrelationships between individuals, firms, and countries continue to multiply and grow. So hang on and enjoy the ride.

The United States and the Global Economy

From the previous example, it would be easy to conclude that a large percentage of what is consumed in the United States comes from outside its borders. If you had to guess, what percent do you think it would be: 40 percent, 50 percent, maybe even 75 percent? Any of those answers would be wrong. Does that mean that more than 75 percent of the goods and services Americans consume within their borders is made in other countries and shipped over? The answer is no. According to the U.S. Department of Commerce, in 2006, goods and services from other countries that Americans consumed were equal to about 16 percent of the United States' total economic output. That probably sounds way too low, doesn't it? Read on to see how that number came to be.

Tough Times for Coffee Addicts and Choc-a-holics

What would happen if the United States decided to go it alone and withdrew from the global economy, limiting American consumption to goods and services now produced within our country's borders? Does the prospect bring on visions of deprivation and hardship? For hardcore coffee drinkers, withdrawal symptoms would be immediate, because little coffee is produced in the United States. For most of us, though, the effects would be surprisingly mild.

If Americans could only buy what was produced in America, we would miss out on a number of things we depend on getting from other countries. These include coffee, diamonds, cocoa, silk, tin, and bananas. "Well," you might say, "I could always switch to tea if I absolutely had to." Maybe, but it would be awfully expensive tea. About 50 countries grow the bulk of the world's tea, and America is not among them. India is the world's largest tea producer, and tea is also grown and exported from Sri Lanka, Kenya, and China, to name just a few. In the United States, there is one commercial tea plantation in South Carolina and a few small growers of tea in Hawaii—that's all, folks. So if no more coffee came into the United States and a mass switch to tea occurred, it would drive up the price so much the stuff would be almost like liquid gold.

Kona Coffee from Hawaii is already expensive, but if coffee imports were blocked, Kona prices would jump. Coffee plants from Brazil were planted on the island of Oahu in the 1800s and small coffee farms on Maui, Kauai, Molokai, and Oahu, Hawaii, are currently the only U.S. coffee producers.

As you can see, there is a long list of things for which we depend on others, but for most we would be more irritated than devastated by their absence. Sure, many of us would be a little more tired in the morning, sweet tooths would have less to be satisfied with, and lovers of "bling-bling" would sparkle less brightly, but we would manage to get by.

The problem is that most of the goods in our homes have some components made overseas. Even something as simple as pencils are made from raw materials from around the world, and made with knowledge and skills spread around the world. If U.S. borders somehow became impermeable, the economy could adjust over time, but lots of goods and services now made overseas would have to be produced in the U.S. The adjustment process would consume time and money and pull thousands or millions away from current occupations.

Did You Know?

According to FAOSTAT, the United States imports over 40 spices, with vanilla beans, black and white pepper, capsicums, sesame seed, cinnamon, mustard, and oregano making up three quarters of spice imports. Spices flow to America from over 50 countries, with Indonesia, Mexico, India, Canada, and China providing over half of imported spices.

The U.S. produces 40 percent of its own spice consumption, and exports spices as well, mainly capsicum peppers, mustard seed, dehydrated onion and garlic, and herbs.

"Getting by" would mean having fewer choices in a lot of areas. German and Japanese cars would no longer roll off the car lots—except for BMWs, Mercedes, Toyotas, Nissans, and Hondas now made in America. However, U.S., Japanese, and

German cars made in America contain plenty of parts not made in America. The Jeep Wrangler has over 80 percent of its parts made in the United States, but the Chrysler PT Cruiser has a lower domestic content than the 70 percent U.S./Canadian parts in the Toyota Avalon built in Kentucky.

Our favorite television shows could not be viewed on South Korean televisions. French wines and cheeses would disappear from fine dining establishments. Austrian skis would slip out of your grasp. Fruit smoothies would have to be made without bananas.

Also consider what would happen if things produced in the United States could not meet consumer demand and could no longer be supplemented by imports. For example, 56 percent of the oil consumed in the United States is imported. Should we discontinue bringing it in from other countries, we would still have oil of our own to burn, but prices would rise rapidly, as would trucking and manufacturing costs. As a result, price hikes would ripple across the economy, making many other goods and services more expensive as well.

Go with the Flow

There are four kinds of economic flows that connect members of the global economy to each other.

EconoTalk

An **import** is a good or service produced in a foreign country and brought into a country for consumers to purchase. An **export** is a good or service produced in one country and sent to a foreign country for that country's consumers to purchase.

- **Goods and Services Flows**   The United States *imports* goods and services from other countries and *exports* goods and services to other countries. Though we hear a lot about who wins and who loses in the process of trade, those on both sides must believe they benefit if trade flows are to continue in the future.

- **Capital and Labor Flows**   Members of the global labor force move from one country to another in search of the best employment opportunities (though immigration restrictions limit such movement). Similarly, foreign firms invest capital, in the form of production facilities in the United States, and U.S. firms do the same thing in other countries. In both cases, the goal is to "set up" where capital can be used most efficiently and profitably.

♦ **Information and Technology Flows**   With the explosion in Internet usage in recent years, information flows between countries have increased exponentially, from changes in interest rates to investment opportunities to descriptions of products. And whether transmitted online or in tangible form, technology created in the United States is used abroad while foreign technology is imported for use in the United States.

♦ **Financial Flows**   From paying for imports, buying foreign assets, making interest payments, and providing foreign aid, money constantly flows between countries.

So capital, labor, and finance flow between countries, along with goods and services. Technology and communication advances help coordinate the production, distribution, and marketing processes.

People Who Need People

Countries around the world vary widely in terms of how much their economies depend on exports and imports, though few match the United States' ability to meet so many of its own needs independently. In recent decades, the rapid economic growth of small Asian countries with few natural resources and dependence on trade—Hong Kong, Singapore, Taiwan, and South Korea—have confirmed that though natural resources are handy, countries can prosper without them.

EconoTalk

Gross Domestic Product (GDP) is the total market value of the goods and services produced during a specific year within the boundaries of a country. It includes production by both domestic- and foreign-owned concerns.

The following table shows samples of selected countries whose exports vary widely as a percentage of their *Gross Domestic Product (GDP)*.

The relatively low export figure for the United States does not mean Americans are uninterested in selling goods and services to other nations, or that these products are undesirable beyond our borders. The United States possesses a wealth of wide-ranging resources and can produce most of what its citizens desire. With high incomes at their disposal, American consumers are able to purchase the bulk of what their country produces.

Exports of Goods and Services as a Percentage of GDP (2004)

Country	Percent
Hong Kong	193
Luxembourg	146
Swaziland	84
Ireland	80
Hungary	64
Saudi Arabia	53
Israel	44
Bolivia	31
France	26
Ethiopia	19
Brazil	18
United States	11

Source: World Bank

In terms of volume, however, the United States exports an enormous amount of goods and services. This is because the American economy is the biggest in the world, so that a small percentage of it is still going to be bigger than a much larger percentage of other economies. America's role as an exporter has declined in recent years. In 1950, a full third of the world's exports came from the United States. Today that figure stands at about an eighth. This is not because the American economy has shrunk or become less productive or competitive, but simply because other countries, especially large emerging economies such as China and Japan, have dramatically increased their exports. (Plus, during World War II, most German and Japanese factories, along with English and French factories, were destroyed. Along with a few much smaller advanced economies like Switzerland and Sweden, U.S. manufacturing capacity was unharmed.)

Following is a list of the total merchandise exports from the top 10 exporting countries. Notice that the United States has been surpassed by Germany as the world's largest exporter, a title held by the American economy for many years. This, too, will probably change before too many years pass. Given the rapid expansion of the Chinese economy and the amounts they export, we can expect them to surpass Germany in the future if current trends continue.

Country	Exports (in Billions of Dollars)
Germany	969.9
United States	904.4
China	762.0
Japan	594.9
Netherlands	402.4
United Kingdom	382.8
Italy	367.2
Canada	359.4
Belgium	334.3

Source: World Trade Organization

Are They the Luckiest People?

Countries with large exports usually import a considerable amount of goods and services. Hong Kong, for example, is a wealthy economy that has benefited tremendously over the years from being an efficient and effective exporter. At the same time, however, Hong Kong, an island with little farmland or natural resources, has to import most of what its citizens desire. So not only do they rely on foreign customers and sources of revenue, they also depend on outside suppliers for basic necessities, such as food and fuel. In contrast, the United States has sectors of its economy (such as agriculture) where overseas sales are a significant portion of their business. According to *The Economist*, the United States imported 36 percent of industrial supplies and 27 percent of consumer goods in 2006, but overall the American economy is more self-sufficient than many other countries.

Warning, Pothole Ahead!

Very often the figures for a country's exports and imports are presented similar to game scores. The impression is given that if your exports are more than your imports, you have "won," similar to winning a basketball game by scoring more points than your opponent. If imports are greater, it's presented as a game loss. The truth is that there is no winning or losing to be found simply by comparing exports and imports.

The United States imports more than it exports. Economists are divided on what this means. One school of thought is that this is the result of a wealthy economy able to afford buying more than it sells. Another school of thought maintains that we are living beyond our means and heading for trouble if the trend continues. We will examine the debate in more detail in the chapters ahead.

Although the United States is no longer the globe's leading exporter, it is the leading importer in dollar terms. This means that Americans constitute a very important market for many foreign economies. Guatemala, for example, would see a drastic fall in their export revenues if Americans stopped buying their coffee beans. This table lists the world's top 10 importers.

Country	Imports (in Billions of Dollars)
United States	1,732.4
Germany	934.0
China	752.0
Japan	535.0
United Kingdom	604.0
France	521.0
Italy	484.0
Netherlands	343.0
Canada	413.0
Belgium	318.7

Source: World Trade Organization

As the World Trades

After declining in the 1930s and early 1940s, global trade has increased steadily since the end of World War II. With economies becoming more and more information-based, we can expect more of the same in the future. As you know from e-mailing and using the Internet, transmitting information can be done in a flash today. Distance, though still an important consideration for tangible goods, does not matter when knowledge is bought and sold. After all, sending a file to somebody on the other side of the world does not take any longer than passing a note to the person in the next cubicle.

In addition to the increase in easily transmitted goods and services based on knowledge, there are some other factors that have supported the growth of global trade, and we will now take a look at them.

Did You Know?

Propelling economic growth is the human desire for more and better things. We have so much more than in the past, because we keep getting better at satisfying our desires—and revealing new desires. Again, Adam Smith gave voice to this many years ago:

"Such is the delicacy of man alone, that no object is produced to his liking. He finds in everything there is need for improvement … The whole industry of human life is employed not in procuring the supply of our three necessities, food, clothes, and lodging, but in procuring the conveniences of it according to the nicety and delicacy of our tastes."

Goods Can Get Here from There

In past centuries, the high costs of transportation limited trade between countries. Not only was transportation expensive, it also required the sacrifice of a lot of time to get from one place to another, combined with all the risks that went with making the journey. Hiking over mountains, trudging through hostile territory, and sailing across the ocean in wooden ships came with plenty of difficulty, discomfort, and sometimes disaster. The further the distance, the higher the risk for travelers and traders.

Throughout the twentieth century and into the twenty-first, advances in transportation have made trade dramatically quicker, cheaper, and safer. The effect is to "shrink" the globe and increase opportunities to profit from trade. Natural gas is piped into the United States from Canada. Diamonds can be flown anywhere by plane quickly. Huge tankers transport oil across oceans. Grain can be shipped through the great lakes and across the sea to any port.

A walk through the produce section of any large grocery store is a great lesson in what is possible when transportation improves. Ginger root from China, peppers from Belize, blueberries from Colombia, pineapples from Ecuador, and artichokes from Mexico are but a few examples from a constantly growing list of what we can count on finding easily. A hundred years ago you would have needed to travel to the countries themselves to get these items, and it would have been a long, slow trip to make just to sample some foreign food.

Can We Talk?

If you are in charge of purchasing for a chain of grocery stores, you can fire up your computer, go online, and get price quotes on beef from Brazil, brie from France, tea from China, and beer from Germany in a flash. Placing an order can be done just as quickly, as can paying the bill after the goods arrive. If you need to talk to a supplier abroad, telephone quality has improved, while costs have dropped considerably. Those same phone lines allow you to fax documents back and forth to your heart's content.

From almost anywhere in the world, you can find out about changing stock prices on the New York Stock Exchange, what the exchange rate is if you need to acquire foreign currency, or interest rates in Asia. If you call your American bank, there is a good chance your call will be routed to a call center in India, a location made possible by falling communication costs.

Across Africa, India, and Indonesia, cell phones are bringing the magic of instant communication across distances to developing countries. The economic benefits for coordinating trade have been enormous. Now poor fishermen locate ports with higher prices, and small growers balancing tomato baskets on their head can find which markets are worth walking to.

For billions across the global economy to coordinate their daily affairs, communication plays a central role. The telegraph was a watershed advance for the world economy. And telephones, faxes, cell phones, the Internet, Blackberries, and Palm Pilots continue to push the global envelope.

Dismantling Trade Barriers

In his paper titled "Growing World Trade: Causes and Consequences," Paul Krugman notes that "global trade recovered and expanded after World War II, but it was not until the 1970s that world merchandise trade passed pre-World War I levels." It was not just the end of the fighting that made it possible, though it certainly helped, but a variety of factors. Following are three of the primary factors:

◆ **Transportation Technology**   Hundreds of years ago, trading with foreign countries often meant journeys lasting months, even years. Crossing an ocean and coming back again was a long, expensive process, and risky, too, because not all the ships at sea made it back to port. Land-based travel was no picnic either. Imagine setting out on a journey with wagons and mules where only a few miles per day could be covered, the weather could be anything from blazing hot, to bone-chilling cold, and, in unsettled territory, anything of value was at risk while being transported. Steamships and railroads rapidly transformed this world beginning in the late 1800s.

Today, enormous oceangoing tankers can transport anything from wheat to televisions to cars across an ocean at a much lower cost, a cost low enough that the goods can still be priced competitively when they arrive. There are specially designed planes that can hold surprisingly large amounts and speed across continents and oceans, making a journey in hours that used to take months. The world hasn't actually become smaller or flatter, but it sure feels that way when things move around in it so much quicker and more efficiently.

◆ **Communications Technology**   Not too many years ago, a phone call to another country, or even another state, was a major expense. Not anymore. Not only can voices be transmitted cheaply, but now information via the Internet can travel anywhere, in almost any quantity, at a tiny fraction of what it used to cost, and arrive there infinitely faster.

◆ **Decline in Restrictions**   Though countries still have industries and goods they protect, and not everybody is open to free trade, in general there are less charges, restrictions, and regulations of goods moving across borders. For example, in 1940, the United States tacked on an extra 37 percent to the cost of foreign goods coming into the country, on average. Today the average charge is 5 percent.

Setting New Places at the Table

Almost every country in the world participates in the global economy to some extent, and the number of participants and their level of involvement have been steadily rising. China, for example, could become a bigger economic powerhouse than the United States by 2040 if its growth rate continues on the same track as the last decade. Bear in mind that with an annual growth rate averaging 9 percent since 1978, their output doubles about every eight years. In contrast the world's largest economy at present, the United States, grows at an average of 3 percent a year. India, too, could soon join the ranks of the world's largest economies and most active global traders.

Singapore, South Korea, and Taiwan are more examples of countries that have emerged as major importers and exporters. Taken together, their exports are greater than traditional powerhouses of France, England, and Italy. Following the collapse of the Soviet Union and communism in Eastern Europe, countries that used to trade mostly with the Soviet Union and each other have broadened their range—countries such as Poland, Estonia, Hungary, Romania, the Czech Republic, and Slovakia.

Who Gets What from Whom?

Speaking of developed and developing economies, let's look at how they perform in sending goods abroad and bringing them in to their own countries:

Goods Sent to ...	In Billions of Dollars
Developed Countries	
Canada	161
Japan	50
Western Europe	154
Australia	13
Developing Countries	
Mexico	97
China	35
Eastern Europe	6
OPEC countries	18

Goods Sent from ...	In Billions of Dollars
Developed Countries	
Canada	213
Japan	121
Western Europe	246
Australia	6

continues

Goods Sent from ...   In Billions of Dollars   (continued)

Developing Countries	
Mexico	136
China	135
Eastern Europe	15
OPEC countries	53

Source: World Bank, 2004

Along with the amounts developed and developing countries send to each other, it is instructive to look at particular countries in more detail. One interesting thing that emerges is that countries don't just ship out one set of things and bring in an entirely different set of things. In real life, there is plenty of mixing-it-up going on, where countries look to niches to specialize in instead of all permutations of a single good or service. Take a look, as an example, at the chief goods the United States sells abroad and buys from foreign countries:

Goods Sold to Other Countries	In Thousands of Dollars
Nuclear reactors, boilers, and parts	182,034,125
Electric machinery (sound equipment, TV equipment, etc.)	145,832,282
Vehicles (except railway or tramway)	92,702,820
Aircraft and spacecraft	66,753,299
Medical or surgical instruments (optic, photo, etc.)	61,891,052
Plastics	42,712,143
Mineral fuel, oil, wax, etc.	34,940,264
Organic chemicals	33,654,324
Pearls, precious stones, precious metals, and coins	31,541,395
Pharmaceutical products	25,236,280

Goods Purchased from Other Countries	In Thousands of Dollars
Mineral fuel, oil, wax, etc.	333,578,333
Nuclear reactors, boilers, and parts	243,946,968
Electric machinery (sound equipment, TV equipment, etc.)	229,154,303
Vehicles (except railway or tramway)	215,378,710
Medical or surgical instruments (optic, photo, etc.)	50,514,211
Pearls, precious stones, precious metals, and coins	44,039,147
Organic chemicals	43,690,926
Pharmaceutical products	42,349,177
Furniture, bedding, etc.	39,788,817
Apparel articles and accessories (not knit)	37,865,889

Source: International Trade Administration, 2006

Manufacturing has grown more sophisticated in recent decades as supply chains have integrated production across borders. Charts showing only exports and imports can't convey the whole story. But charts that do tell the whole story grow mind-bogglingly complex. Chemicals purchased from other countries can be fabricated here into complex assemblies that are shipped back out to be included in car or airplane parts that then are shipped back to the United States. All good news for shipping and air freight companies!

The Least You Need to Know

◆ It is almost impossible to go through a day without making use of a broad range of products that have been designed or made in countries outside your own.

◆ The United States buys more goods from foreign nations than does any other country, but as a percent of its economy, the number is much lower than for most other countries.

◆ Global trade is nothing new; it's just much less expensive today. Countries and groups have been engaged in it for 10,000 years.

◆ Countries do not sell strictly one kind of good and buy another. Most buy and sell a mixture according to the desires of their citizens.

2

What's Economics Got to Do with It?

In This Chapter

◆ As the globe turns

◆ Economies of all shapes and sizes

◆ The entrepreneur's role in global economics

Economics can help us understand and evaluate what individuals and nations are experiencing as their economies become more integrated. Economics is a way of thinking that yields valuable and unexpected insights about what takes up a large part of most people's lives: producing and consuming goods and services.

To kick off our examination of economic principles, here is a definition of economics provided by the British economist Lionel Robbins in 1932: "Economics is a science which studies human behavior as a relationship between ends and scarce means which have alternative uses." Economics is not a physical science where it is possible to conduct experiments whose outcomes can be predicted and repeated. Humans are too unpredictable for that! But economics does provide us with methods for gathering, organizing, and evaluating knowledge.

The "Dismal Science" Lights Up the Globe

In the mid-nineteenth century, Thomas Carlyle, an English historian, dubbed economics the "dismal science." The label has stuck in the years since, because economists always seem to be the ones telling everybody else that they can't do everything they want and that every move they make involves sacrifice. The reality, however, is that Carlyle opposed the point of view expressed by contemporary economists—such as John Stuart Mill—that all humans (and not just the upper crust) come equipped with the drive to make better lives for themselves and will benefit each other if allowed to pursue their goals freely.

Everybody Is Beautiful in Their Own Way

Even today, similar controversies abound when considering international trade, in particular the question of what individuals and groups will decide what other individuals and groups around the planet should be allowed to buy and sell. Should trade be managed on our behalf by wiser minds, to keep us from wounding each other too badly when we clutch and grab at the goodies in our global superstores?

Economics has always been unique in its faith in the capacity of individuals to act in their own best interest, the conviction that you and I know ourselves best and should therefore not be interfered with—so long as we behave ourselves and obey the law of the land. Rather than being dismal, economics is an optimistic discipline that expresses faith in mankind in all its shades and variations.

You Can't Always Get What You Want—And You Don't Need To!

In economics, scarcity is a constant—there are never enough of the things we want to go around. Have you ever heard somebody say, "Darn it, I have too much money and wish the stuff would stop coming in?" Probably not, and if you ever do you'll surely volunteer to help them get rid of it. And scarcity is not just about material things; for example, seats are scarce in the symphony hall, violin and foreign language lessons are scarce, and so are yoga classes and graduate degrees. All these services take scarce resources to produce and require scarce money and time to purchase.

For example, any parent knows what it's like to face the onslaught of unlimited wants with only *scarce resources* at your disposal. Even if you could buy a child everything she wanted today, by tomorrow a whole new list would be growing, and another one after that. Wants are similar to zombies in horror movies; you can never get rid of all of them.

Humans come equipped with *resources* (such as talent, for example) and can get their hands on other resources (such as land and money) in the quest to satisfy their ends (goals). The challenge, as Lionel Robbins made clear in his definition of economics, is deciding how best to use the resources at our disposal. The possible uses of our resources are endless, but resources themselves are finite.

EconoTalk

The finite amounts of land, labor, capital, and entrepreneurial ability that are never sufficient to satisfy our wants are **scarce resources**.

A **resource** is anything that can be used to produce goods and services and includes everything from oil and water to employees and computers.

Continuing our example, parents seeking to satisfy at least part of their children's endless want lists do the sensible thing: they focus on using their resources to make the best living they can, then trade their labor, via money, for the things they hope will temporarily satisfy the wants they and their children have. It is this quest to satisfy our wants with finite resources (making choices in response to scarcity) that is the heart of economics and also what drives globalization.

Do You Really Know What's Best for Yourself?

In addition to scarce resources and unlimited wants, economists also assume that individuals have *bounded rationality*. A rational person is one who acts in her own best interest, which translates into making choices to improve well-being. The obvious problem here is that anybody who pays attention knows that people sometimes do things that make them worse off, or make choices that appear to have no rational basis (remember leisure suits?).

Economists assume individuals are approximately rational. Allowing for all our limitations and faults, people as a rule act in their own best interest, at least as they see it. Of course, buying a shirt made in China might not seem rational to the American textile worker whose job was eliminated because retailers and consumers are buying clothing made abroad.

EconoTalk

Bounded rationality is a term introduced by economist Herbert Simon describing the way individuals acquire, process, and interpret information with limited capacities.

The Push to Profit

Whether an individual is investing scarce resources of time or money, their rational goal is to benefit as much as possible. Economists call gains beyond just wages for work or rent for assets *profit*. After all, with limited resources, we seek out the best "bang for the buck." Milton Friedman, a Nobel Prize–winning economist, famously said "There is no such thing as a free lunch." For every lunch, no matter who picks up the tab, somebody planted and grew crops, harvested them, and brought them to market, where someone else purchased, packaged, and transported them to the restaurant to be prepared and served. A list of people all signed on to the project (a list longer than the menu), and each acted for personal gain—each had the rational goal of supporting themselves and their families.

Warning, Pothole Ahead!

Profit motive is an individual's incentive to gain something extra, beyond just wages or savings account interest. Some entrepreneurial souls try starting new businesses, or buying in bulk and reselling in smaller quantities, or buying concert tickets (or condos) early to resell later at hopefully higher prices. Profits are about more than money. The saint who helps shelter the homeless and the cold-blooded bond trader both have profits in mind—that is, gains over and above the effort they invest.

This is actually a key insight for modern global economies: we don't know the names of the hundreds or thousands who labor to prepare our food, stitch our clothes, make our furniture, and construct our shelter. In 1900, three out of five Americans lived in small towns or rural communities where they knew by name most of those they exchanged goods and services with. What is amazing in the modern world is that we so easily benefit from vast knowledge distributed across the globe, from how to grow particular foods and spices, locate and mine minerals, cut and sew, design and assemble, carve and shape, program and debug, and all the vast range of skills that few of us possess but most of us use in finished products each day.

The small slice of time all these people devoted to our "free lunch" was time they sacrificed from other tasks, so even if we didn't pick up the tab, our lunch had a cost paid by people working together around the world. Entrepreneurs along the way gain profits through innovations that lead to better-tasting or less expensive lunches.

Any kind of profit calls for giving up something first. People seek out the best prospects for making profits. And if the grass looks greener on the other side of the fence, or on the other side of the border, is it any wonder that more and more people go there to graze?

The Future Is Now

No matter how we decide to invest our resources, we won't know how well the decision pans out until later. Even though we can't predict the future, we do make decisions now based on projections of what the future will be like.

Economist John Maynard Keynes spoke of the role expectations play in economics. He said there are waves of pessimism and optimism about the future that heavily influence decisions made in the present. For example, when everyone seemed to believe that housing prices could only go up, they stretched financially to purchase a first or bigger house (and many stretched further to purchase a second and third house). During the dot.com boom, tech stocks seemed only to rise. But at some point, optimism led investors to overshoot the mark. First tech stocks fell to Earth, and recently home prices have been falling.

The point here is that the payoffs people think will or will not happen in the days ahead have a lot to do with where, when, and how much we invest. Opportunities with great potential attract great sacrifices of limited resources. Those with little or no apparent potential attract none. One thing that concerned Keynes is that people weren't always rational in what they expected—that "animal spirits" could influence us in ways that didn't make much sense and could be bad for the economy.

Did You Know?

Writing in *The General Theory* (1937), economist John Maynard Keynes said, "… most of our decisions to do something positive … can only be taken as the result of animal spirits—a spontaneous urge to action rather than inaction."

In the years since Keynes, economists have added the assumption of rationality to his ideas on expectations. This means that, though none of us can predict the future, we can develop rational predictions about what might happen and act on them in the present. One example of this was developed by Milton Friedman. He looked at how people spent money and surmised that their purchases of things such as homes were based on estimates of what they would earn in the future and not just on their earnings at present.

Did You Know?

Rational expectations theory tells us that individuals and firms adjust their decisions in response to changes in economic policy, which may result in the policy becoming ineffective.

Trying to Up the Average

The global economy is vastly varied. Some of us were born in economies that were developed over a century ago. Others—most of the globe—live where investment, industrialization, and international trade have arrived only recently or not at all. We find far different daily lives for citizens in different countries of the global economy. Following are average incomes for the citizens of different countries. As you read through the data, and then read the chapters that follow, think about possible reasons for the differences.

Average Income for a Sampling of Nations (2005)

Country	Income in Dollars per Capita
Switzerland	48,230
United States	41,400
Japan	37,180
France	30,090
South Korea	13,980
Mexico	6,770
Brazil	3,090
China	1,290
Pakistan	600
Nigeria	390
Rwanda	220
Liberia	110

Source: World Bank

Income in dollars gives us only one dimension, though an important one, of what life must be like around the world. Average income doesn't tell us who enjoys the most flavorful meals or the most tranquil domestic lives, or who hikes the most scenic trails. For example, the average worker in the United States in 1907 made much less money, and most lived in small towns. Life was worse in many ways (visiting the dentist, for example), but not all. By 1957, average wages had risen and dentistry had improved. And both are even more improved in 2007. But that doesn't necessarily mean that people were happier in 1957 than 1907 or that today's wealthier people are happier—just that society has advanced.

In the Beginning

In terms of historical time, it hasn't been very long that humans have had much of anything to do with each other outside of small groups of related members, let alone developing a global economy. Approximately 10,000 years ago, members of these roving bands of hunter-gatherers discovered that trading with each other could make everybody better off.

This was an enormous step forward. Back then life was nasty, brutal, and very short (with an average life span of about 29 years). Even basic resources such as food were in short supply, and simply surviving from day to day was a real challenge. With so little to go around, it's no wonder that different groups of humans did not interact (at least, not positively) with each other. Why give something to somebody from a foreign group if you and yours might not have enough to get by?

Did You Know?

Humans are the only creatures who cooperate with each other outside of their groups but within their species. Adam Smith observed, "Nobody ever saw a dog make a fair and deliberate exchange of one bone for another with another dog ...."

The answer turned out to be that if you shared something you were good at making or doing, you could get something in return the other guys specialized in. Suddenly both groups improved their lot in life and things got a little less nasty, brutal, and short. Of course, to do that each side had to trust that if they gave, not only would they get in return, but they would also profit from the exchange.

The amazing changes in human interactions that made globalization (and any kind of economy at all) possible is extremely well-documented in Paul Seabright's 2004 book, *The Company of Strangers.* As he narrates in wonderful detail, small groups of related hunter-gatherers cooperated with each other in fighting and hunting, but were very careful and untrusting when around "foreign" groups.

For trade to work among the hunter-gatherers, humans had to rely on their capacity for rational calculation (making deals in their best interest) and an instinct for reciprocity, which meant rewarding good behavior (fair deals) and punishing bad behavior (ripping off somebody who trusted you to trade fairly).

Examples abound of groups mistrusting each other and especially outsiders. The economic evidence, however, clearly shows that cooperation beyond rigid, narrow boundaries is the best prescription for improved well-being.

The ancient Greeks believed the gods would punish those who harmed strangers. From Homer, we learn the Greeks were called upon to offer a meal to strangers before even asking their names. Such traditions encouraged trade, as traveling merchants naturally preferred to bring their wares to Greek villages (for a good meal!).

Warning, Pothole Ahead!

Though competition is an important factor in the study of global economics, cooperation is much more important. Sure, beating out the other team might be fun, but having each side focusing on how best to earn rewards by satisfying the wants of the other team gets you much further ahead.

Enter the Entrepreneur

Successful entrepreneurs understand that rewards go to those who do the best job of anticipating, meeting, and even creating wants; they understand that ongoing success means offering buyers extra value. Entrepreneurs are alert to opportunities to create this extra value with better service, new products, and new combinations of goods and services. Strong coffee in many "flavors" was around long before Starbuck's. Panera Bread creates a want for tastier European breads and pastries by baking and presenting them in attractive surroundings. European coffee and bread have been around for centuries. Why have they only recently become popular in the United States?

The Rewards of Playing Nice

The foundation of any healthy economy or individual interaction is the process of mutually beneficial exchange. Would you go to a restaurant again if the food was terrible the first time? Would the restaurant owner continue serving customers if she lost money every time somebody walked in the door? In less-than-healthy economies, consumers expect to be cheated. Metro, an international supermarket chain, opened its store in Vietnam with tomatoes neatly wrapped in plastic. Consumers ripped the plastic open since they assumed the rotten tomatoes would be hidden under the good-looking ones on top. In China, Metro learned fish labeled "fresh" wouldn't sell. Metro officials learned that in China "fresh" means "alive"—so now Metro's Shanghai store features giant fish tanks.

A great thing about this is that the only (legal) way to advance ourselves is by doing good for others, be they at home or elsewhere. Not only did economics promote diversity before diversity was cool, it gave us the golden rule before we knew what gold was!

Did You Know? _____

Microeconomics examines decisions made by individuals, households, and firms, and those made in markets for specific goods and services.

Macroeconomics is concerned with the economy as a whole and the major components of it, such as all household, business, and government sectors.

Little Picture, Big Picture

Be it selling lemonade to thirsty joggers from a driveway stand or selling software to strangers thousands of miles away, mutually beneficial exchange is the cornerstone of the process. What brings the little picture into focus does the same when the lens gets bigger.

When we study global economics, everything gets thrown in the mix. So although we are concerned with how a country does overall in its dealings with other nations, we also pay attention to what is happening with particular goods and sets of individuals.

Nobody Plays for Free

Speaking of particular goods and individuals, one of the reasons studying the incomes of different countries is useful is because these incomes are resources that can be used to obtain other things. No matter where you go, lunch is never free, and in some places you get a lot less on your plate than others.

Referring back to the incomes in the previous table, average individuals in those countries have limits on what they can spend. In each case, they must decide how to allocate these incomes to obtain the best combination of goods and services. To illustrate, let's use a simple model where an individual can buy only two different things—meals at $10 each and CDs at $20 each. If his income is $180, the following combinations are possible:

Meals	CDs	Total Dollars Spent
18	0	180
16	1	180
14	2	180
12	3	180
10	4	180
8	5	180
6	6	180
4	7	180
2	8	180
0	9	180

As you can see, the possible combinations range from lots to eat and no music to nothing to eat and plenty of music. Most people settle on a point somewhere in between the extremes, but total income dictates where those boundaries are set. No matter the income, though, there are always *opportunity costs*. In the preceding table, you can see them clearly. If you want to buy four instead of three CDs with your money, you must give up two meals. Should your stomach win out, every two meals down the hatch means a CD you will not own.

EconoTalk

The value of the next best alternative, the one given up to make another choice, is the **opportunity cost**.

The Shift to Services

Earlier in this chapter, we went over the different resource categories of land, labor, capital, and entrepreneurial ability. As economies the world over become increasingly information- and service-based, traditional resources such as land become less important as people power becomes more important. For densely populated cities in the Philippines, India, or Kenya, people are the most valuable resource for modern economies. Far more income can be earned in light industry or call centers than from guiding plows behind oxen or fishing from wooden boats. Entrepreneurial ability has become valuable as developing countries begin to organize and develop new enterprises to compete in the world market.

Out with the Old, In with the New

Economies benefit from entrepreneurship when new products are introduced that appeal to consumers, whether domestic or foreign. With revenues going up as a result of successful innovation, new jobs are created and wealth increases, which means average incomes go up and the budget constraints move to higher levels. If you refer back to the previous table, for example, when income rises from $180 to $240, consumers can increase their consumption of meals, CDs, or a combination of the two choices.

But as income rises, consumers don't just buy more of the same goods and services. Instead, they usually purchase new goods and services, and what they buy is influenced by entrepreneurs eager to make new goods and services popular and profitable. Wealthier consumers can afford iPods and Zunes, for example. But these shiny new products have been bad news for CDs, as consumers discover they can download new music and skip visits to music stores. A rising tide may lift all boats, but some established goods and services get thrown overboard in the process.

Did You Know? _____

Joseph Schumpeter, an Austrian economist, introduced the term *creative destruction* in the mid-1920s to describe the entrepreneurial, free-market process where new goods and services replaced older, less desirable services. It's easy to understand why established firms try to restrain the new, creative alternatives—these more modern ventures threaten established products or ways of doing business.

Entrepreneurial Reform: Estonia's Success

On the heels of the Soviet Union's dissolution, the Eastern European country of Estonia sought to introduce free-market, entrepreneurial reforms in its economy. Within a few years, Estonia went from being a poor country with high unemployment to one with a blazing 11 percent rate of economic growth and hardly any unemployment. Their citizens now vote online in elections and have a 24 percent flat-tax so simple that their annual tax returns can be completed in a matter of minutes.

How did Estonia do it? Soon after escaping Soviet control, they transformed their economy from one run by the government to one determined largely by individuals and firms. Regulation was scaled back and simplified, citizens were encouraged to be entrepreneurial, and their property was protected by a strong system of laws. In 2004, after having been almost completely dependent on the Soviet Union for trade in the past, they were one of Eastern Europe's most prosperous countries—only 4 percent of their growing trade was with Russia. Not only that, they had become a member of NATO and the European Union.

Matt Laar, the Estonian Prime Minster, based his reforms on the single economics book he had read—Milton Friedman's *Free to Choose.* Laar commented recently, "I was so ignorant at the time that I thought that what Friedman wrote about the benefits of privatization, the flat tax and the abolition of all customs rights, was the result of economic reforms that had been put into practice in the West. It seemed common sense to me and, as I thought it had already been done everywhere, I simply introduced it in Estonia, despite warnings from Estonian economists that it could not be done. They said it was as impossible as walking on water. We did it: we just walked on the water because we did not know that it was impossible."

The Least You Need to Know

- Economics is the "science of choice" and is relevant whenever individuals with scarce resources are trying to make the best decision from an unlimited array of alternatives.

- In economics, it is assumed that individuals are approximately rational beings capable of acting in their best interest.

- Nothing comes to us for free. All choices and actions require the sacrifice of limited resources and giving up opportunities not taken.

- The process of mutually beneficial exchange became common practice after our ancestors witnessed the benefits that followed.

- Entrepreneurs cause wealth to increase by introducing new goods and services to economic markets.

Making Markets with the Invisible Hand

In This Chapter

◆ Introducing supply and demand

◆ Buyers and sellers look for harmony

◆ The mysteries of prices

Demand, supply, prices, competition, and innovation shape not only how much of a particular good or service is sold in small markets, such as roadside flower stands, but also do the same for products sold globally. Global markets are more complicated, of course, but the song remains the same.

Going to the Market

Have you ever been to a farmer's market? Sellers of fruits, vegetables, meats, cheeses, and lots more gather in one place to make their goods available to customers. Sellers, acting out of self-interest, want to sell their products for the highest possible price. Buyers, also acting out of self-interest, want to buy at the lowest possible price. Neither sellers nor buyers are going to get everything they want, but they can work out mutually beneficial deals that allow them to leave the market better off than they were when they entered. Such is the magic of markets!

Little Pond, Big Pond

In everyday life, people participate in many markets, both as buyers and sellers. You sell your labor at work and then go out to a hotdog stand to purchase your lunch from a vendor. In exchange for giving up a big chunk or your time, talent, and energy at work, you seek the best combination of high pay and rewarding work. When you set out for lunch, you want to get the best meal for the least outlay of money and time.

EconoTalk

In a **market economy,** the decisions made by buyers and sellers coordinate the allocation of resources.

Economies that allow such markets in labor and lunches to function relatively freely are called, not surprisingly, *market economies.* How else could an economy work, you might wonder? Well in China for a time, the government decided it would be better, certainly more social, if everyone were to eat together at large communal meals. Government officials also assigned jobs and decided wages. It seemed to work for a while, but the ultimate results were unfortunate, to say the least.

As the process of globalization has accelerated, we are all now involved in markets that include buyers and sellers from around the world. Everybody wants the best deal, whether they are getting paid or doing the paying, and the opportunities increase as new markets open worldwide. When China opened to world trade, 1 billion new consumers and producers began gradually integrating into the world economy, all interested in better jobs and better goods and services.

Wither Your Wares?

As we get deeper into how markets function, keep in mind that, although economic markets are efficient, they are not going to yield results that everybody is happy with. For example, pretend you have developed a new hot sauce recipe and develop a mail-order business where you fill orders from around the world. Sales are booming and you are making piles of money. Others notice your success. Suddenly, a gaggle of competitors slap together similar recipes and open their own mail-order business, except they charge significantly less money. If their products catch on, you must now cut prices to keep selling your sauce.

Say you do that, then a foreign-owned business with low-wage employees to brew and bottle and access to cheaper ingredients comes along with a similar sauce that is even cheaper. Would it bother you that the competition has advantages you do not possess? Would you want to "level the playing field"? Could you blame consumers for saving money by switching to the cheaper sauce? Participants in this sauce market have good reasons for the decisions they make, but that doesn't make it easy.

You may remember the television advertisements Texas picante sauce company Pace ran making fun of picante sauce imported from "New York City." Cowboys around a campfire find out they are being served imported sauce. Authentic picante sauce, the advertisement emphasizes, is from Texas, not made in another state and definitely not shipped in from another country.

Does it matter where similar-quality products are from? Can cowboys, or anyone else, tell the difference between Texas and New York City picante sauce? Well, that is a matter for consumers to decide. Advertisers sometimes try to help them make the decision to buy domestic goods. Other advertisers push consumers to buy imported goods.

But the question for many is whether buying domestic helps the economy or buying foreign-made goods causes harm.

Who's In Charge Here?

If more than one vendor is selling apples, for example, and the apples are approximately the same size and quality, vendors will adjust their prices so that they all eventually charge the same amount. This price will be the lowest that allows vendors to maximize their sales, sell off their inventory, and earn enough of a return on their investment to continue selling apples.

Apple vendors, of course, don't particularly like being "price takers"—that is, being stuck making only enough to get by selling the same apples other vendors are selling. So they search for new varieties of apples to offer, or branch out into caramel apples and other extras consumers might be willing to pay for.

Fruit and vegetable markets are actually pretty interesting (at least if you are an economist!). They work in an amazingly smooth manner without most of us noticing. Local fruit tends to ripen and get trucked to market at the same time each year. This huge increase in supply is communicated to consumers through lower prices and increased advertising. At harvest time, large fruit displays often greet shoppers as they enter the local supermarket. But how does anyone figure out the exact price to charge?

Store managers have trucks off-loading fruit at harvest time and know they have only a few days to convince shoppers to carry it all out the front door. And they know nearby markets are also flush with fruit at harvest time. It is a sophisticated dance where changing prices coordinate with changing supplies and influence how much and what kind of fruits are served in homes across the country.

You might think applesauce, canned peaches, and strawberry jam are just everyday consumer goods. They are, however, a way to solve the harvest-time problem of very low prices. Every fall, homemade and factory canning and jam-making take advantage of low harvest prices to set aside fruit for year-round consumption.

Though it sounds counterintuitive, markets work most efficiently when the members are allowed to direct them through the cumulative effect of their decisions (the invisible hand). If an "apple czar" was appointed to run the market and decided what could be charged and how much could be bought and sold, it would be awfully difficult for this person to acquire and process the information necessary to beat the cumulative decision-making power of the market.

An apple czar might decree that everyone eat more apples and make applesauce at harvest time. But prices accomplish the same end because they keep falling until apple markets clear.

A challenge arises where members of a market have the ability to manipulate it. For example, say these apples have been tainted with an unhealthy substance, but apple growers get together and keep that information under wraps. Now the market can't function at maximum efficiency because it lacks important information, and this can lead to *market failure*. But in withholding knowledge of tainted goods, producers would be defrauding stores (claiming their products are safe when they aren't). And in doing this they would be up against grocery store chains (and their lawyers) who have strong incentives not to poison their customers. Regulators and trial lawyers also have their own ways to encourage food safety.

EconoTalk

When a market does not bring about the best overall allocation of resources, a **market failure** has occurred.

Or local apple growers might get together to withhold apples from the market, keeping prices higher at harvest time (and maybe making their own applesauce). Of course, they still have to compete with local peaches, bananas, and grapes, as well as apple growers willing to ship their apples from nearby regions.

Making Demands

With our unlimited wants and limited resources, we want to give up as little as possible for the most in return. Picture yourself in a grocery store, hungry for food but with only a few dollars in your pocket. What to do? Make a beeline for whatever does the best job of being cheap, filling, and decent tasting. You'll pass more desirable food along the way, but given your wants and the few dollars in your pocket, the caviar gets ignored in favor of the five-for-a-dollar boxes of macaroni and cheese.

Not Just a Theory, It's a Law

If you go to a Happy Hour, you'll see a good example of demand in action. Lower-priced drinks mean more are purchased, and at a time less popular for drinking (which is why bar and restaurant owners choose earlier times for Happy Hours when their bars would otherwise be mostly empty). Consider, also, an all-you-can-eat buffet, where one price is paid and customers can eat all they want. What happens? People pile their plates high and go back for more; for the more they eat, the less it costs them per bite. They are making the most of their money.

When drink prices rise after Happy Hour winds down, drink consumption goes down, just as food consumption declines after the buffet ends and customers are charged per item.

The *law of demand* states that the less an item costs, if everything else remains equal, the more of it will be purchased. The law of demand also states that the more an item costs, keeping everything else equal, the less of it will be purchased. To test the law, ask yourself these questions: Have I ever bought more of something solely because the price went up? Have I ever bought less of something solely because the price went down?

Here's a simple illustration of demand:

>   **Law of Demand**
>
> $P\uparrow Q_D\downarrow$
>
> $P\downarrow Q_D\uparrow$
>
>   P = Price; Q_D = Quantity demanded

A Demand Curve Slopes Down

We've all seen pictures of demand curves. They slope down and to the right and simply show us that as prices fall, people are willing to purchase more. Each point on the curve represents a different combination of price and quantity.

Example of a demand curve.

To explain the demand curve, consider the following schedule showing how many bagels will be purchased at different prices.

Price per Bagel	Bagels Demanded (Purchased) Daily
1.25	100
1.00	200
.75	350
.50	550
.25	800

The demand curve doesn't tell us what the market price is or will be, just how many bagels consumers will buy at different prices. It is also important to understand that the demand shown does not reflect how many bagels customers want to buy, but how many they are willing to buy at each given price. At $1.25, 100 bagels were purchased, an amount that rises to 550 when the price is lowered to $.50.

There must also be a specific time period for a demand curve, such as a day, week, or year. There is a big difference between selling 350 bagels in a day versus taking a year to sell that many. Whatever the time period, there is always an inverse relationship between price charged and the amount purchased (demanded): when price goes up, bagels demanded goes down; when price goes down, bagels demanded goes up.

Warning, Pothole Ahead!

Though a demand curve shows us how much of a good or service will be purchased at different prices, that is all it shows us. If anything besides price changes, such as consumer tastes or competing products, a new curve is needed to reflect the change.

When the Curve Shifts

What happens when something other than price changes and demand is altered? Instead of moving along the curve, we have to construct a new curve. As a general rule, something that causes an item to become more desirable (consumers will pay more for each unit) will cause the curve to move up and to the right. If an item becomes less desirable, the curve moves down to the left.

Considering the bagel example previously, when the bagels become more desirable, the curve will move up to the right. If the bagels become less desirable, the curve will move down to the left.

Price per Bagel	Original Bagels Demanded Daily	Demand Shift! Krispy Kreme™ Opens Next Door— Estimated New Bagel Demand
1.25	100	75
1.00	200	150
.75	350	250
.50	550	400
.25	800	600

The Demand Variations

What are the factors, apart from price, that cause a new demand curve to be generated? Let's take a look at the most prominent of them:

- **An increase in buyers:** If more people want to buy a product, maybe because it is now available in more countries, the total amount demanded and revenue generated will increase even if the price doesn't change. The rise in consumers can drive up prices because when more buyers are competing for the same amount of goods, prices rise and that item goes to those who want it enough to pay more.

- **Consumer taste:** Tastes change constantly. What is desirable today may be out of fashion tomorrow. For example, if your peppermint bagels strike a chord with bagel-buyers everywhere, the fact that more consumers prefer them and want to buy more will cause the price to rise. If it suddenly happens that bagel-buyers turn against peppermint, less of these flavored bagels will be bought and prices will fall.

- **Change in income:** For most *normal goods*, demand goes up as incomes do. A poor town where workers can only afford bagels on holidays might start buying them regularly when a new factory moves into town and provides better-paying jobs. If the factory shuts down, though, it's bye-bye bagels and back to *inferior goods* such as cereal or toast.

EconoTalk

Products where demand rises and falls with incomes are **normal goods**. Those products that consumers purchase less of when their incomes rise and more of when their incomes fall are **inferior goods**.

Goods that are used together are **complements**. Goods that can be used in place of each other are **substitutes**.

- ***Substitutes* and *complements*:** Not only do changes in taste and income affect demand, the prices and desirability of other products have an income also. If consumers start buying more bagels, then things such as cream cheese that commonly go with them will also experience an increase in demand, or a decrease if bagels decline in popularity. At the same time, if goods that can be consumed instead of bagels, such as scones and croissants, become cheaper and more desirable, the demand for bagels goes down. If these things become more expensive or less desirable, bagel consumption goes up.

- **Expectations:** Consumers also make buying decisions based on what they expect to happen in the future. If you have a bagel-loving customer who thinks bagel prices are going up soon, she might buy a lot more than usual to stock up. If this customer thinks bagel prices are going down, she may hold off on bagel purchases until they become cheaper.

Expectations apply to bagel sellers also. If you anticipate huge increases in your sales, maybe you'll buy that new Mercedes now instead of waiting. Should it appear to you that bagel sales are headed into a hole, you might save the dough now, even though sales are good, so you have some set aside when the market declines.

The Supply Side

Having demands doesn't do us much good unless there are suppliers of the things we desire. Purchasers in normal markets want to buy at the lowest price, and buyers want to sell at the highest price. As a result, prices have a lot to do with how much gets supplied and even what is supplied. Higher demand for bagels bids wheat supplies away from donut makers or other wheat buyers.

Not Just Another Theory, It's Another Law

Because suppliers want to get the best possible deal when they exchange their resources, we can predict what happens when prices change.

The *law of supply* states that providers of a product will make more products available for sale when the prices that can be charged rise. The law of supply also states that less of a product will be made available when the price that can be charged for it drops.

Following is a simple illustration of supply:

> **Law of Supply**
>
> $P\uparrow Q_s\uparrow$
>
> $P\downarrow Q_s\downarrow$
>
> P = Price; Q_s = Quantity supplied

Not only are suppliers anxious to get the highest prices for their goods, they often have to charge more because, if labor or materials are becoming scarce, their costs can rise when production increases beyond a certain point.

As with purchasers, producers of goods and services have other opportunities available to them. They need to cover their product-related costs and want to earn more producing whatever they are engaged in producing than they could making anything else.

Peaking Behind the Supply Curve

A supply curve is simply a series of points where we can see how much producers will make available to buyers at different prices. We move up along the supply curve as prices rise because more is made available when consumers are willing to pay more.

> /////// **Warning, Pothole Ahead!**
>
> The supply curve only tells us how much will be purchased at different prices. If anything else changes, a new supply curve must be drawn.

Example of a supply curve.

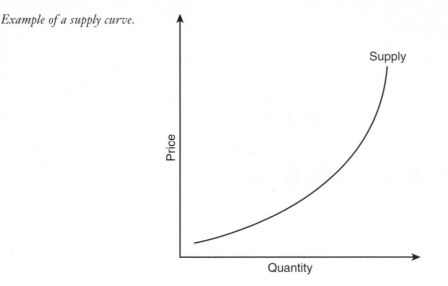

What Makes the Supply Curve Shift?

Now let's have a look at the common things that call for a new supply curve when they change.

- **Prices of resources:** If the costs of labor, materials, management, or anything else that goes into a product rises, the cost to produce it also rises. At current market prices firms don't make what they used to per item, so either they will make do with less at the same price or charge more for it. If these costs go down, firms (though it may not be their first choice), especially in a competitive market, will lower their prices.

- **Technology:** If a new or improved process makes it possible to produce more of a good with the same resource inputs, the cost per item will go down.

- **Cost of other goods:** If similar or competing goods go down, this will put downward pressure on a good. This can work in the other direction if there is a price rise.

- **Number of sellers:** Usually an increase in the number of sellers of a good causes the supply to increase, with a price decrease following. If the number of sellers goes down and supply does, too, expect prices to rise.

- **Taxes:** A rise in business taxes causes prices to go up. A reduction in taxes causes prices of goods supplied to go down.

- **Expectations:** What a supplier thinks is going to happen in the future influences what is charged. If, for example, they expect a decline in resource prices, they may take advantage of it now by lowering prices and gaining a larger share of the market. If, on the other hand, they predict an increase in taxes, they may raise prices now.

Equilibrium: Finding Balance in Compromise

Despite having conflicting interests, buyers and sellers generally settle on prices that benefit both. Both are price searchers in market transactions—that is, sellers want higher prices but don't quite know what they can get, and buyers want lower prices but don't quite know what they will have to pay. Often there is a certain amount of posturing and pretending before both sides discover the price that works to move the most goods. This is often called the equilibrium price.

Give a Little Bit

For all we hear about competition, cooperation is at least as important, especially when it comes to setting equilibrium prices. For this process to work, however, a number of conditions have to work.

For starters, markets should be open, so any party can enter or leave at will. Markets work best when all relevant information is freely available and the products being sold can be made by lots of producers.

There aren't a lot of markets where these conditions exist in pristine form, but in markets that are mostly open we can come close, which is often good enough. Competition and innovation regularly push prices around, and markets for even everyday products like pencils and pens seem ever changing.

Clearing the Shelves

At equilibrium, competition among sellers has driven prices down to just enough to cover costs but no more. When economists talk about costs, they don't mean just the costs involved in producing a good or service, but also the opportunity cost for the seller. This is the amount the seller could earn if his or her assets were safe, sound, and making interest in a savings account.

Buyers have various preferences; for example, a new pen that one buyer would pay $3 for, other buyers might pay only $1. This frustrates sellers who would like to get that extra $2 from buyers willing to pay. Generally, though, sellers pick a price that makes the most profit (sales times price). When buyers get a pen for $1 they would have paid $3 for, economists call that "consumer surplus." There is a natural limit to how much consumers will purchase because, even at a good price, there are other things they want to spend their limited resources of money on. Markets generally "clear" because buyers and sellers keep on exchanging goods and services until sellers have sold and buyers have purchased all they want. In the real world there is usually stuff still left on the shelves after business is done for the day, or empty shelves that were not stocked with enough for every customer (competent employees and managers tend to notice mistakes and try to adjust tomorrow's prices and orders). Markets, when allowed to function, do come surprisingly close to the economic description of equilibrium.

In Search of a New Equilibrium Point

Economists in the classroom like to work with supply and demand curves and graph equilibrium points. But when factors such as tastes, material costs, availability, and endless others change, supply or demand graphs tend to be yesterday's news. In the classroom, new equilibrium points are instant. In the real world it takes longer for market players to gather and process the new information.

For example, with gasoline prices high and fears that the growing demand will lead to shortages and even higher prices—not to mention the environmental impact—companies and countries, along with a great many inventors, work hard to develop alternatives to gasoline. Brazil, for example, has mostly transitioned to ethanol made from sugar, so there's no reason why more countries can't do the same, right?

As we previously learned, the supply and demand curves for a good shift in response to changes in the markets for other goods. With increasing quantities of farmland being used to produce corn for ethanol in the United States, there is less of it for other crops. With the supply of available corn and wheat dropping, prices go up. And it doesn't stop there. When food costs more, less money is left for other goods, and growth can lag as a result. Ethanol and biodiesel can be made from sugar, corn, palm oil, and other crops. When these become more expensive, so do meat, eggs, and candy, among many other things. Higher food prices are felt particularly acutely in India and China, countries with huge, growing populations already consuming more food—at the same time they are consuming more energy.

According to Moody's Economy.com, wholesale food prices from 2006 to 2007 rose by approximately 14 percent in Turkey, 11 percent in India, and 6 percent in China, rates much higher than what had been experienced in recent years. Global grain stocks in 2007 hit their lowest level in 30 years. It has been estimated that 30 percent of American grain will be used in ethanol production by 2008. Sixteen percent was used for ethanol in 2006.

In 2007, corn harvest is projected to be the largest since 1933—13 billion bushels, up 2.5 billion over 2006. Corn for ethanol was 2 billion bushels in 2006, according to the USDA, which projects corn for ethanol to rise to 4 billion bushels by 2011. The key question is how corn farmers will respond to higher prices in expanding their corn production. And as they expand acreage, what resources will they draw from other crop production?

The surge in oil prices over the last couple years pushed ethanol prices up as well (especially with federal subsidies for ethanol). Higher prices kicked off a construction boom for new ethanol processing plants, and a corresponding increase in demand for corn to feed hungry ethanol plants. Higher demand for corn pushed corn prices up, and farmers with land that could be planted in corn noticed. The result? U.S. farmers planted 93 million acres of corn in 2007, nearly 20 percent more than last year, and according to the USDA, the largest crop in 63 years.

What Do Prices Tell Us?

Prices incorporate a lot of information, usually more than any one person or group could possibly be aware of or interpret accurately. Say there is a poor garlic harvest this year and, at the same time, consumers become convinced that eating huge quantities of it will cure anything that ails them. The poor garlic harvest reduces supply and causes garlic prices to rise. The increased popularity of garlic causes a further rise in price because demand goes up. The person convinced garlic is the key to health benefits may not know anything about the bad garlic harvest, but higher prices reflect it, and her willingness to pay more makes sense given the higher value of garlic to her. Those less convinced that garlic matters can pass on it.

Whither Justice?

In the example above, garlic lovers who are low on money and have other important things to buy are out of luck when prices rise. To them, higher market prices feel cold and unfair. Economic markets are very good at incorporating information and matching up supply with demand (and getting both sides to compromise), but markets address justice only as a process (that is, when buyers and sellers are honest and honor contracts). The results that follow from the market process may seem quite unfair, especially to those that lose out. It doesn't seem fair when a particular farmer's garlic crop is wiped out by floods, or when garlic prices are pushed below his costs by unexpected imported garlic. That is not the sort of cosmic unfairness markets can remedy. Just as the driver of an old, beat-up car might badly want the Mercedes that costs four times what he earns annually, garlic lovers short on cash are out of luck. They can save up for these purchases, try to get a better-paying job, or pray that a rich uncle appears bearing a brand-new Mercedes with a trunk packed with garlic, but the market itself—an amalgam in this case of thousands of Mercedes and garlic producers and consumers—won't budge unless it has to.

Doling Out the Goodies

In many cases, such as health care for example, markets can be budged. Medical care is provided for those who cannot afford to pay for it, money is provided for those unable to find a job, and food is given to those who cannot afford any. Nonprofit organizations provide these services, and the government does, too. The disagreements about interfering with market functions start when we look at theories of how entire markets or economies might be managed. As you will see in Chapter 18, there are significant differences in how economies function depending on how free or directed their component markets are.

The Least You Need to Know

- ◆ Economic markets are mechanisms that allow buyers and sellers to exchange resources.

- ◆ For economic markets to function, both consumers and suppliers often have to settle for less than they want.

- ◆ Markets do not function in isolation. Changes in tastes, resource availability, competition, related products, and many other things can dramatically change market results.

- ◆ Prices are very efficient reflections of information but they have nothing to do with subjective notions of justice or fairness.

Part 2

Zero-Sum Games Are for Losers

Those that expect to be hurt by trade push for political protection. Taxes on imports, called tariffs, protect some but do so at the expense of the general public. Just as it makes sense to purchase goods we cannot make easily at home, it makes sense to import goods made better or cheaper abroad. And even a country best at producing everything would benefit from trade, since it is the relative production skills that drive trade, which economists call "comparative advantage."

This part looks at why global trade, rather than being a competition in which winners win at the expense of losers, is a process than can enrich all nations involved. Not all is rosy, however; some individuals do lose, and not all countries benefit equally.

"Tell me again why we care about
the new numbers for the Chinese trade surplus?"

Chapter 4

From Resources to Riches

In This Chapter

- ◆ Countries with resources finding riches or ruin
- ◆ Distributing revenues
- ◆ Developing better resources

As more people in more countries join in international trade, the scope of trade deepens. More people in more places contribute their special skills and their region's special advantages in resources, climate, and culture. But do these trade advantages just appear at random? What role do institutions, firms, and individuals play in identifying and developing regional resources? We'll answer those questions in this chapter.

Use It or Lose It

Chinese firms are enormous producers of clothing because they have a vast supply of inexpensive labor. Brazilian producers sell many, many tons of coffee around the globe because they have plenty of land and the right climate for it. Canadian farmers export bushels of wheat by the billions because they have the endless plains to grow so much of it. In each case, firms are taking advantage of resources in regions that provide clear advantages and sources of economic strength.

The Snowflake Variations

As with individuals and snowflakes, no two regions or countries are identical, and nowhere is this more apparent than in resource endowments. The most successful members of the global economy are those where entrepreneurs and enterprises have opportunities to develop local resources and discover comparative advantages in world trade. Where government agencies or established firms restrict or heavily regulate new competition, prosperity lags. In trade theories of earlier centuries, labor was regarded as the primary cost of production. Things have changed. Have you heard the saying, "Behind every great man is a woman?" Now you can add the following: "Behind every highly productive worker is a machine."

Happiness Is a Warm Machine

The countries reporting the highest productivity per hour worked closely resembles the list of countries with the most capital invested per person, capital resources that enable workers to produce high-quality goods faster.

Remember the old saying, "You have to spend money to make money?" In the case of worker productivity it is true, and it isn't just the productivity-boosting equipment that money has to be spent on; it's also the workers who run the machines. To see how this point translates into real life, look at the difference in hourly pay in the next table. The United States is set at 100, which means countries with a higher score pay employees more and those with a lower score pay employees less. In both cases, think of the numbers as percents of American pay.

Percentages for Hourly Compensation in Comparison to the United States

Country	% of American Compensation
Norway	128
Germany	118
Switzerland	113
United States	100
Japan	88
United Kingdom	82
Canada	75
Israel	57

South Korea	43
Hong Kong	27
Mexico	11

Source: United States Department of Labor

The Wealth in Institutions

Much as Michael Jordan's astonishing coordination made him wealthy, coordination from well-functioning legal systems is key to wealth production in countries, whether or not firms have local natural resources to draw upon. Research by Kirk Hamilton of the World Bank shows both natural resources and existing factories and infrastructure account for only 20 percent of wealth in developed countries and 40 percent in developing countries.

Most wealth in the world, Hamilton argues, is in social institutions: "Human capital and the value of institutions (as measured by rule of law)." Hamilton calls this *intangible capital*, a hard-to-measure collection of people's "knowledge and skills; and the level of trust in a society and the quality of its formal and informal institutions." Worldwide, Hamilton argues intangible capital constitutes over three quarters of total wealth.

The World Bank has a rule-of-law index that tries to measure the strength of legal institutions people have confidence in and adhere to. Some countries, like Switzerland, rate high (98 out of 100), while others, like Nigeria, rate very low (5.8). The World Bank study concludes: "Rich countries are largely rich because of the skills of their populations and the quality of the institutions supporting economic activity."

A Balancing Act

Alas, unlike diamonds, comparative advantages are not forever, at least at the same level. Why is it that being able to produce something at a lower level of sacrifice (opportunity cost) cannot be maintained into infinity and beyond? The economists who developed the *factor endowment theory*, also called the Heckscher-Ohlin theory, had an explanation.

EconoTalk

The **factor endowment theory** states that differences between countries in comparative advantage can be explained by the variations in resources they have available and make use of.

As these Swedish economists developed their theory in the 1920s and 1930s, they added the assertion that comparative advantages would decline or disappear over time as countries traded with each other. The reason is that a country taking advantage of an inexpensive factor that is in plentiful supply (such as labor or lumber) will use a lot of it, which causes demand for it to go up. And from our discussion of the law of demand in Chapter 3, do you remember what happens when demand increases? That's right—price also goes up, and that means the advantage is not so great anymore.

Bear in mind that this doesn't happen the second a country begins trading. A developing country with millions of eager workers, for example, is going to have to employ quite a few of them before wages go up, and there might be plenty of room for pay to increase before their comparative advantage evaporates.

Warning, Pothole Ahead!

Many things predicted by economic theories, such as a steady equilibrium point or the equalization of costs between countries over time, do not work out so neatly in reality. The simplifications are made for illustration, not because economists believe the world will follow "the letter of the law."

The process can be sped up, however, if labor is being used to produce enough of a product that its price drops at the same time labor costs increase. A firm may find itself caught between the pincers of rising costs and falling revenues. Eventually it may come to pass that it costs just as much for one country to produce something as the country it has profited from selling it to.

If China, for example, takes full advantage of its supply of workers in producing textiles, their pay will rise. At the same time, the wages of American workers who have fewer job opportunities in the industry will drop. The wages of comparable workers in both countries won't be exactly the same, though closer, but the opportunity costs of China and the United States in the production of clothing would move toward each other.

By referring back to the previous table, you will observe a common phenomenon: the real world does not arrange itself according to theory. If it did, hourly compensation for manufacturing workers would not vary so much by location.

Staying in Practice

California wines are doing the unthinkable and catching up with the French. Germany is no longer the only country to look to for top-flight luxury cars, nor is it the only place in the world to find great beer. Things change as countries develop new ways to make the most of what they have.

At the same time, there are areas of trade where it seems to be, "The more things change, the more they stay the same." Following is a table that lists the top 10 American exports to China and the top 10 Chinese exports to America. Notice that, as Heckscher-Ohlin would predict, American exports are concentrated in higher-skill areas that require greater capital investments (equipment, machinery, know-how) whereas China has a higher percentage in things that are more labor-intensive. Notice, however, that neither country is restricted to one type of production.

Top 10 American Exports to China (2004)	Price in Millions of Dollars
Boilers, machinery	4,109,132
Electrical machinery	3,950,078
Aircraft, spacecraft	3,428,793
Medical instruments	1,258,610
Plastics	995,157
Agricultural products	917,873
Fertilizers	666,331
Chemicals	618,408
Iron and steel	494,006
Rawhides	441,625

Top 10 Chinese Exports to America (2004)	Price in Millions of Dollars
Sound equipment, televisions	24,203,918
Boilers, machinery	20,214,882
Toys, games, sporting goods	14,440,857
Footwear	10,226,857
Furniture, bedding	9,922,790
Apparel	4,478,787
Leather products	3,909,098
Plastics	3,227,957
Photo, optical equipment	2,758,628
Iron and steel	2,108,719

Source: United States Department of Commerce

Who Gets Paid?

Global trade increases the incomes of people in countries who participate, which is why they get involved in the first place, but the spoils are not spread out evenly. As discussed in the beginning of this chapter, globalizing economies can count on having some members who see their standard of living decline. So let's have a look at how the revenues from trade are distributed within countries.

Is One Man's Advantage Another Man's Curse?

The American economy has a large workforce of skilled workers, so it makes sense for the U.S. firms to focus on making and selling goods that draw on this resource. U.S. firms trade these goods and services for others that require less skill to develop and make. But what about American workers who do not possess this kind of skill set—whose jobs of choice overlap with those that can be done in other countries for less money? For example, making leather goods is a skill workers in China can master. You can see from the preceding tables that a lot of rawhides are exported to China and imported again as finished leather goods. Skilled American workers in the leather-goods industry have a hard time competing with skilled Chinese workers with much lower living standards.

Wages of Americans with in-demand skills have risen steadily, but the pay for unskilled work hardly budges. The prospects for the future are not any better. As millions more low-skill workers join the labor force in China, India, Africa, and Latin America, the products they can produce inexpensively overseas tend to displace or push wages down for low-skill American workers making similar products.

Once upon a time in the United States, it was possible for a high school graduate with no high-level skills to get a job at a company such as General Motors or Kodak that was secure, paid well, and came with generous benefits. Today, most of these jobs have either disappeared or, where they do exist, demand significantly more training and continued skill development.

Learning to Earn

It is no wonder that American companies and workers in traditional sectors of the economy such as automotive, steel, and textile production often come out in favor of restricting imports from other countries. Sure, Americans who buy cheaper clothes, steel, and cars may be better off, but many Americans who used to make those products and haven't found other work at similar pay are worse off.

In 1973, the average worker with a college education earned $1.48 for every $1 earned by a worker with a high school education. Thirty years later, in 2003, the gap had increased to $1.85 for the college-educated worker for each $1 earned by the high school–educated worker. This is a trend likely to continue far into the future. During the same 30-year period, imports as a percentage of the economy also increased, so it is easy to view evil outsiders as the source of this growing wage gap, but imports actually account for only a small percentage of it. In a 1997 study for the Institute for International Economics, Trade and Income Distribution, William Cline measured the causes of the 18 percent increase in the wage gap between skilled and unskilled American workers that occurred between 1973 and 1993. The top six factors stated as the percentage impact are:

Factor	Percent
Skill-biased technological change	29
Unexplained	29
International trade	7
Stagnant minimum wage	5
Decline of labor unions	3
Immigration	2

As you can see, technological change is much more influential than trade with foreign countries or foreign workers entering the country. In other words, things would not improve a lot for unskilled American workers if we sealed the borders and kept all foreign workers and foreign products out. The problem does not lie beyond American shores, but squarely within them—Made In America.

It is worth noting, too, that income disparities are not arbitrary; instead, they reflect growing differences in productivity between college-educated workers and those with just a high school education. The major role of technology suggests the reason—sophisticated machinery can now do more of the repetitive work that skilled and semi-skilled assembly and service workers used to do. Knowledgeable phone company and credit industry workers who used to answer our telephone calls have been widely replaced with voice recognition systems that can answer many of the easy and basic questions from callers.

Most importantly, in many advanced economies the real earnings of unskilled workers is rising, though not as fast as earnings of skilled workers. This raises the questions asked in a recent World Bank study: "Should society care about the absolute well-being of workers, which globalization enhances, or should it worry about their relative well-being? If it is the latter, do you want to stop technological changes as well?"

A Slap from the Invisible Hand

If we remember the laws of supply and demand from Chapter 3, the situation for unskilled American workers is made clear. Demand for skilled workers has risen, and wages have increased accordingly. But wages fell for unskilled workers as resources shifted to support higher-skilled labor. A dozen autoworkers trained in robotics can substitute for hundreds of workers who used to handle labor-intensive tasks. Even if the number of jobs for unskilled workers remained steady, a fall in wages is still possible. Why is that? Competition from foreign producers means domestic companies cut costs to compete, which means wages can fall simply to keep existing jobs. In recent years, the pressure to reduce pay to Ford, GM, and Chrysler autoworkers—as increasing market share is lost to companies such as Toyota, who produce cars in southern states as well as overseas—is a good real-world example.

Where the Endowments Roam

Long gone are the days when a firm's most valuable assets came in the form of tangible assets such as land, building, and equipment. Twenty-first-century firms, except for the few who have managed to maintain traditional ways of doing business, have their most valuable assets in employee knowledge, networks, and skills. Estimates range up to 70 percent for the average value of a company that comes from the talents of its employees. Economists call this *human capital*. Just as sophisticated machinery raised productivity in manufacturing, so knowledge workers with sophisticated know-how raise productivity across America's expanding service economy.

EconoTalk

Human capital is the productive value of education, training, experience, talent, health, and other resources possessed by workers.

In the nineteenth century, even in industrialized nations, only a small percentage of workers in any business had completed high school, and an even smaller percentage had gone to college. As the twentieth century progressed, however, there was a boom in education, and the educational profile of the workforce changed dramatically. In developed nations, it has become more and more difficult to thrive with a nineteenth-century–level education in the twenty-first century.

Following is a list of selected countries and the percent of the workforce who have participated in different levels of education. Note that postsecondary education is a broader category than is often assumed, including technical schools, colleges, and universities.

Country	% Primary	% Secondary	% Postsecondary
United States	100	96	81
Germany	100	95	31
China	100	70	53
Russia	100	88	49
Mexico	100	66	31
Cambodia	99	39	23
Chile	90	85	43
Chad	48	18	14
Ethiopia	35	25	36

Source: World Bank, Human Development Report, 2004

In the developing economies of the world, demand for higher levels of education, both in levels of overall participation and levels completed, is increasing because of the clear payoffs that follow for individuals and nations alike. Remember, though, education does not just mean spending time in colleges or universities: any setting that provides training in skills that are in demand provide the same effect.

Warning, Pothole Ahead!

By itself, the number of years spent in school does not guarantee an increase in job security or pay. The key is to build a skill set you can exchange for a healthy salary. Showing up at an employer's door with a degree that enables you to perform a function they stopped performing years ago is not a recipe for success.

Building on Strengths

When the different factor endowments of nations are examined, it is interesting to note how those of capital, skilled labor, and unskilled labor are distributed. Capital resources and skills are heavily concentrated in a few countries, which (no surprise) are also most of the wealthiest. Higher concentrations of unskilled labor (again, no surprise) go with less wealth.

The following table summarizes more of the findings reported by Cline for the Institute for International Economics.

Factor Endowments as Percentages of the World's Total

Country	% Capital	% Skilled Labor	% Unskilled Labor
United States	20.8	19.4	2.6
European Union	20.7	13.3	6.9
Japan	10.5	8.2	2.9
China	8.3	21.7	30.4
India	3.0	7.1	15.3
Mexico	2.3	1.2	1.4
Canada	2.0	1.7	0.6

Good to the Last Drop

If your grandmother ever told you, "Anything worth doing is worth doing well," she could also have been addressing countries specializing in the production of certain goods and services. The point is that as a country produces more of something they get better at it and gain efficiency, which means their costs of production drop and they have the chance to make, sell, and profit more than in the past. Not only does the producing country benefit, but if prices go down when costs do, all those who purchase their wares also benefit. Economists call it *economy of scale*.

EconoTalk

An **economy of scale** happens when a firm that increases their output of a product is able to lower their cost per unit at higher production levels.

Here's an example: pretend that you and a group of friends went into the chocolate chip cookie business last year and have been steadily building up sales all over the globe. In the beginning, it cost you a dollar to make each premium cookie. Then things began to change. As your firm gained experience, new techniques were developed that cut down on the labor time required. Then you discovered a cheaper chip supplier; you then found a less expensive way to advertise and ship the cookies. What happened here is natural: your cookie company learned from experience and used that knowledge to become more efficient.

From there, let's say the Crooked Cookie Company invests in new machinery that spits out cookies at a faster pace. Again, costs drop. Maybe you figure out how to eliminate some steps in the production process and learn how to operate with less inventory on hand. More gains are had from improvements in technology. So long as firms and countries are experiencing economies of scale, it usually makes sense to keep ramping up production (assuming demand will match it).

> **Warning, Pothole Ahead!**
>
> Though diamonds are forever, economies of scale are not. It's possible for a firm to increase production to the point where the increase in size makes them less efficient and causes costs to rise. This is a diseconomy of scale—a state you want to avoid.

When Demand Begot Demand

An oversimplification of comparative advantage could easily lead one to believe that countries abandon production of the kinds of goods they import and focus on making things they can sell to other countries who, in turn, have given up making these in favor of trading for them. In reality, the wealthy industrial nations conduct most of their trade with each other—consumers who have similar tastes.

Not surprisingly, people in developed countries have preferences that overlap. They tend to produce and purchase similar kinds of cars, clothes, and gadgets. An individual out shopping for a new car in the average American city, for example, can choose from a Ford, BMW, GMC, Subaru, Chrysler, Toyota, and a few others. For the most part, the choices differ, but each brand targets customers with similar tastes and levels of income.

Riding the Cycle Out

Many manufactured goods have similar life cycles—stages that products pass through where they go from being new, innovative, and unique to common and copied. Following are five general stages, though there is plenty of room for variation:

1. A new good is introduced to the home (domestic) market.

2. The product demonstrates strength as an export.

3. Foreign production of the good begins.

4. The domestic producer loses its competitive advantage.

5. Competition from imports is established and grows.

The results for a good, then, can vary quite a bit depending at which stage they are in. Take the Crooked Cookie Company as an example again. In the beginning, your cookie is introduced to local consumers and they see that it is good. Word spreads of these remarkable treats and you can't ship enough overseas to meet demand. It makes sense now to start making the cookies in the countries where demand is greatest, so new factories are built and baking begins.

Competitors' mouths water at the sales of Crooked Cookies, and they wrack their brains in an attempt to make one just as good. They get closer and closer, and pretty soon the demand for their product, Straight and Narrow Cookies, takes off. Not only do they compete with your firm abroad, but before long these cookies start popping up right next to yours on grocery store shelves. No longer are you the new kid on the block; now you are the mature matron trying to hold on while the youngsters push and shove all around you. And that's the way the cookie crumbles. (Who could resist?)

The Least You Need to Know

◆ Globalization is not responsible for the growing wage gap between skilled and unskilled workers. This gap results from advances in technology.

◆ Although global trade makes the world a wealthier place overall, not everybody experiences the same benefits, and many industries and individuals experience a decline in well-being.

◆ Today and in the future, the most successful nations in the global economy will be those with the best-developed human resources.

Chapter 5

Can Second Best Be Good Enough?

In This Chapter

- The fallacy of trade as a zero-sum game
- Making the world safe for tortoises
- The gains from trade
- As the dance card fills

In Chapter 1, we covered the basics of economics and learned that the market process of mutually beneficial exchange allows people and economies to become much better off than they would be without it. In Chapter 2, we discovered that this was the very process that enabled mankind to move beyond the limitations of a hunter-gatherer existence and begin cooperating outside the boundaries of small groups, thereby allowing all groups to become better off from trade between former enemies. If all this is so clear, why is there so much controversy surrounding global trade?

The answer is that although exchanging goods and services across the planet makes people richer overall, not everyone benefits equally. For example, in the beautiful Blue Ridge mountains in southwest Virginia, there is a town whose biggest employers used to be textile and furniture factories, but no more. In 2006, three factories located in Galax shut down. As a result, more than 1,000 people—about 17 percent of the town's workforce—lost their jobs.

Trying to convince newly unemployed sawyers and gluers living in Galax that globalization is a good thing would be a hard sell. American retailers who found cheaper suppliers in China might well pass along cost savings to their customers, but those benefits are spread out over a wide range of customers who each benefit only modestly. The pain from job losses, both financial and psychological, is much more intense for individuals and families, and tends to be concentrated in local communities. Plant closings and large-scale layoffs, and the concentrated suffering they bring, is more noticed and newsworthy than small gains diffused throughout the larger population.

Zero-Sum Games

Trade between countries is often portrayed as similar to a basketball game—one team has more points when the game ends and wins, while the other team has fewer points and loses. But global economic relations are not just about who "scores" the most, and the fact that one country's economy does well does not mean that another's must do poorly, as in a *zero-sum game*.

EconoTalk

In a **zero-sum game**, the benefits to one individual or group are offset by losses to others, which means that there is no overall gain for everybody as a whole from playing.

With all the emphasis put on competition and winners and losers, it is easy to lose sight of the fact that economic markets prosper when the majority of the participants are enriched by "playing" with each other (exchanging goods and services). Envision a basketball game where both teams win (okay, one team might win more than the other, but both are still better off for being on the court together) and know that they will continue to win so long as they keep playing by the rules.

Can't Win for Losing: The Mercantilists

From about the sixteenth to the nineteenth century, there was a popular school of thought in Europe called *mercantilism*. In their writings, the mercantilists made the case that a country would become wealthier if it sold more to other countries than it bought from them. To make sure this happened, the mercantilists said that the government should regulate trade to discourage imports and encourage exports.

The mercantilists said that, when more was sold to foreigners than foreigners sold to the mother country, the increased inflows of gold and silver would enrich the country and enable citizens to produce more and have more. Trade surpluses were good and trade deficits were bad. The standard of living for the fortunate country would rise and keep rising in the future, so long as they held true to the course.

> **Warning, Pothole Ahead!**
>
> Just because a country's exports are more than their imports does not mean they are better off. And when exports are less than imports, they are not necessarily worse off either.

As with many simple things that sound good but don't work out so well, mercantilism had some problems. In the eighteenth century, Scottish philosopher and economist David Hume pointed out it was only possible to have a positive balance of trade (sell more to others than you bought from them) for a limited period of time. His reasoning takes us back to supply and demand: as more gold and silver flowed into the high-selling country, the increase in the amount of money would cause prices to go up. And guess what? When prices of domestic items increased, competing goods offered from other countries began looking more attractive. Consumers, always looking for the best deal, would begin buying more foreign goods and eliminate the trade surplus.

The Bad Idea That Refuses to Die

But wait! Couldn't a country's government simply pass a law saying that its citizens could only sell their wares to "outsiders" and not buy any in return? As we will see in later chapters, this has been attempted over and over again, both for particular industries and segments and entire economies, but it never seems to work out as well as planned. To begin with, how many other countries are going to keep tolerating the one who only wants to sell and never buy? Not only that, but the stubborn country will keep driving its own prices up for citizens and drastically reduce their choices.

Mercantilism rests on the belief that trading with other countries is a zero-sum game, which means that they view the world's total wealth as a set amount. No wonder they advocated grabbing everybody else's money—if the pie is never going to get bigger, then cut out the biggest slice you can! Following Hume, Adam Smith issued a powerful challenge to mercantilism in his book *The Wealth of Nations* (1776).

Did You Know? _____

In the 2007 *Index of Economic Freedom*—which ranks countries according to their levels of economic freedom—the *Heritage Foundation,* in conjunction with *The Wall Street Journal,* ranked the six most free economies and the six most repressed. Note that the freest economies are among the world's wealthiest, and the most repressed among the poorest:

Top Six Countries for Economic Freedom: Hong Kong, Singapore, Australia, United States, New Zealand, United Kingdom.

Six Most Economically Repressed Countries: North Korea, Cuba, Libya, Zimbabwe, Burma, Turkmenistan.

Adam Smith explained that the world's wealth is not an amount that has to remain the same. It can be increased and, further, the best way to increase it is for all countries, companies, and individuals to specialize in what they do best and trade for the rest. (How's that for a little economic rhyme?) The gains from using our limited resources more efficiently will then benefit everybody involved. From today's perspective, it seems so obvious that specialization increases wealth. Bear in mind, though, that the bulk of the gains from specialization (both in wealth and health) have happened since *The Wealth of Nations* was published. The world was a much different place when the mercantilists were trying to sell their way into a superior spot in it.

Somebody Has to Be #1

Even though *The Wealth of Nations* came out more than 230 years ago, Adam Smith's argument in favor of free trade is still not understood well. It is not that people are too dense, but that Smith was looking at a bigger picture than most of us do in our day-to-day lives. Bear in mind that he never had to worry about an economist from a foreign land coming along and replacing him, so he could afford it. It took another economist, David Ricardo, to fully unveil the benefits of free trade, but he, too, is often misunderstood.

Leader of the Pack

Adam Smith's model about free trade's benefits was simple. The underlying idea was that everybody should focus on what they do better than others and then trade from strength. In a world where resources are always limited, it makes sense for people to stick with what they can do more efficiently (at a lower cost) than others. This translates into "more bang for the buck" when it comes to using up those resources. According to Smith, one country able to produce something more cheaply than another could be the result of expertise, experience, climate, or any other talent or resource that provides a special edge.

Divvying Up the Duties

What Adam Smith was speaking about is the same thing that humans discovered 10,000 years ago when they moved beyond the boundaries of small groups and began trading with each other. Though there would be no sightings of economists for thousands of years, people realized they could enjoy a bigger pie if they focused on what they were good at making and traded for the rest.

The following table is an example of *absolute advantage*. We have a simple world where two simple countries each produce two simple products: chicken wings and wing sauce. Note the relative strengths and weaknesses of each.

 EconoTalk

A country has an **absolute advantage** when it can produce a good more cheaply than another country.

Output per Labor Hour

Country	Chicken Wings	Bottles of Hot Sauce
Chickenland	80	20
Roostertopia	25	40

If the countries don't have anything to do with each other, Chickenland can produce either 80 wings per hour or 20 bottles of hot sauce per hour, and Roostertopia can produce 25 wings per hour or 40 bottles of hot sauce. It is obvious that Chickenland has an advantage when it comes to chicken wings and Roostertopia has the advantage with hot sauce. If they join forces and let each one produce what they have absolute advantages in, they can both trade for the other item, and both countries come out ahead. Of course, with more wings and hot sauce available for everybody, they now need a third country to produce an antacid.

Somebody Has to Bring Up the Rear

Absolute advantage works out just fine in a world where each country has a superior niche, but what if your country happens to be one that cannot manage to do anything better than anybody else at all—basically, there is no absolute advantage to be had? Does that mean the rest of the world will trade with each other but leave one untalented nation out in the cold, a global orphan? Fortunately, that does not have to be the case. And that is where David Ricardo comes in.

Early in the 1800s, England had a set of rules called the Corn Laws that restricted the import of various agricultural goods from foreign countries. The intent was to protect English landowners from the competition of producers abroad who could grow and sell agricultural products more cheaply. David Ricardo, an economist, opposed the restrictions and pointed out that even if England's corn sales, for example, went down, the country would not be harmed in the long run because limited resources would be freed up that could be devoted to produce and sell more profitable goods.

 EconoTalk

Comparative advantage exists when one country can produce a good or service at a lower opportunity cost than another.

Because Ricardo's points and the theory of *comparative advantage* are a little trickier to grasp than absolute advantage, let's start with the more intuitive example. Say that you can mow the lawn in one hour and your kid can mow the lawn in two hours. You have the absolute advantage. But what if you could also fix a leaky gas valve in that hour while your kid watched cartoons during the same hour? Fixing the leaky gas valve and keeping the house from blowing up is obviously a much more valuable use of your hour than mowing the lawn (and let's say you can only do one or the other, not one and then the other). In other words, the opportunity cost of you mowing the lawn is the possible explosion of your home, while the opportunity cost of the kid mowing the lawn is a bunch of silly cartoons. Because the kid is sacrificing much less by mowing the lawn than you (has a much lower opportunity cost), it makes sense for the child to push the lawnmower—even though you are twice as fast at it—and leave you to save the family from a fiery death.

And now for the official example. Fast forward from the earlier table to a time when Roostertopia has developed the means to open up an absolute-advantage lead in both chicken wings and hot sauce.

Output per Labor Hour

Country	Chicken Wings	Bottles of Hot Sauce
Chickenland	80	20
Roostertopia	90	40

At this point, Chickenland might feel as though the sky is falling, but such is not the case. Roostertopia is now more efficient at both products, but it doesn't make sense to stop trading with Chickenland. The reason is that even though they are now better at chicken wings, every hour they devote to producing them means sacrificing an hour when they could be producing the hot sauce they have an even greater advantage in. Both countries benefit overall if Roostertopia keeps its eye on the sauce and leaves the wings to the other bird.

Warning, Pothole Ahead!

Even if a country is no longer, or never was, superior at producing a good or service in comparison to other members of the global community, it does not mean they have no chance at succeeding with it. The key to successful trade lies in finding ways to make contributions that call for less sacrifice than others have to make.

And the Last Shall Be First

The real world, packed with many different countries putting out a wide variety of goods and services, is much more complicated than the simple examples of absolute and comparative advantage previously shown, but the principles still hold and are the reasons why countries, each seeking to do the best for themselves, continue to engage in global trade at steadily increasing rates.

What we see the world over is a complicated matrix of countries seeking out partners who they can benefit from trading with, given each side's cluster of absolute and comparative advantages.

Whatever array of absolute and comparative advantages exist at one time, place, or both, do not assume they remain that way forever. As technology advances and innovation proceeds, new sources of advantage are constantly springing up. For example, with the cost of telephone communication being driven down drastically over the last few years, there has been rapid growth in the number of call centers in India and Latin America. If you call your bank for account information, the Midwestern accent you might have heard on the other end is replaced by a polite voice from New Delhi.

All of a sudden, a country with a plentiful labor supply and a growing number of workers who speak English becomes a desirable place to locate a call center when technological advances remove distance as a discouraging factor. The same holds true for writing computer programs. With work that can be transmitted back and forth across oceans via the Internet at minimal cost, programmers in India, who work for half of what Americans with similar abilities do, can begin to do the programming grunt work supporting both American and Indian IT (Information Technology) companies. And over time, programming skills in India will rise to compete with top U.S. programmers, much as the overseas cookie producers of the last chapter did.

Did You Know? _____

In 2000, the country of Bangladesh turned some heads by selling $175 million worth of hats to the United States. According to the theory of comparative advantage, this makes plenty of sense: Bangladesh does not have a sophisticated manufacturing base, but does have plenty of unskilled workers who want jobs. What is also interesting here is that hats have become a specialty of sorts for them. Pakistan, a country similar in its endowments, exported $130 million worth of sheets to the United States but only $700,000 of hats in 2000.

The Gains from Trade

As advantages, opportunities, and opportunity costs change, new avenues of trade open up. Though it's not easy for a country to see a former strength being whittled away by companies thousands of miles away, the process releases labor, land, capital, and entrepreneurs to search for and develop alternative projects.

Earlier in the chapter, we looked at the town of Galax. As traumatic as losing jobs to Chinese competitors was, most of the displaced workers found new employment. Some, such as one who trained to become an x-ray technician and another who opened up a gourmet coffee business, even managed to make better livings. But older workers and those with fewer skills or less flexibility for relocating had a harder time and some gave up trying to replace the job they lost, even with a lower-paying one.

Speaking of lower pay, the loss of a job to foreign competitors who may help the rest of us save money when shopping is often replaced by one that does not pay as well or does not come with the same level of benefits (another form of a pay cut). In the 1980s and 1990s, most Americans who worked in manufacturing but lost their jobs to foreign competitors were employed again within a few months, but most had to take a pay cut, and 25 percent saw their pay drop by more than 30 percent.

More for You, More for Me

What would happen if a law was passed in the United States banning coffee imports? At present the only American coffee produced comes from Hawaii, so that state would have a terrific incentive to raise production all it could. After all, there are millions of coffee addicts willing to pay as much as they are able to keep those fixes coming. Hawaii wouldn't be able to produce enough coffee for all Americans, so other warm parts of the country would be given over to attempts at coffee bean growing and huge greenhouses would probably start popping up all over.

So what would happen when you strolled into your neighborhood coffee shop to feed your habit? It would cost a lot more and, unless you were both wealthy and extremely passionate about coffee, the amount you drink would drop significantly.

After coffee drinkers from across the United States unite and force the coffee bean restrictions to be lifted, imports will quickly rise and prices will fall, and we can go back to being as jittery as ever.

Gains and Pains

Despite all the worries about jobs and industries being lost to foreign competitors who capitalize on sources of comparative advantage, advances in technology—especially in the United States—have a much bigger impact on the economic landscape.

Since 2000, the United States has lost approximately 3.1 million manufacturing jobs. They all went to China, right? Wrong. In the same period, China lost even more manufacturing jobs: 4.5 million. Who is swiping all those jobs? Nobody. Well, robots maybe, and better, faster assembly lines. Manufacturing production, the actual amount of goods made in both countries, has increased during the same period, and the reason is simply that we have become more productive and can increase output with fewer workers than were needed in the past.

Consider this: 9 of the top 10 manufacturing countries, who account for 75 percent of what is made in the world, have lost jobs in the last few years. The lone exception is Italy. In the United States, total employment in manufacturing stands at around 14.2 million jobs, which is the lowest it has been in more than 50 years. Does this mean we are counting on sweatshops to produce everything? Not yet. Since 2001, manufacturing productivity (what can be produced per hour of labor) has gone up by 24 percent.

Did You Know?

In an average year, the American economy destroys 30,000,000 jobs and creates nearly 31,000,000 jobs.

Doing more with fewer people is nothing new. In 1900, 41 percent of the American population worked in agriculture. Now that figure stands at 2 percent—and we produce a lot more food now than we did then. Additional examples abound. In 1970, 421,000 people worked in telecommunications, doing things such as manning switchboards where they handled around 9.8 billion calls a year. Not too shabby, right? But compare those figures to today, when 78,000 operators handle 100 billion calls in a year, and long-distance calling costs a small fraction of what it used to.

With these huge reductions in specific industries, one could be excused for assuming that there must be a chronic lack of good jobs today, but such is not the case. The unemployment rate as of the end of 2006 stood at 4.5 percent, low by historical standards, and the economy is having no problem creating new jobs. The technology that taketh away giveth more—so far.

The Least You Need to Know

- Global trade is not a zero-sum game. The process of mutually beneficial exchange between countries raises the overall level of wealth.

- There is a strong, positive relationship between openness to trade with other countries and the incomes enjoyed by citizens of open countries.

- Every time a country or industry devotes resources to producing a particular good or service, the cost can be measured by the value of the opportunities given up.

- Technological advances within the United States have caused much more unskilled job loss than trade with foreign countries has.

Tariffs, Trade, and Trouble

In This Chapter

- ◆ How do I tax thee? Let me count the ways
- ◆ What the consumer response is to taxes on trade
- ◆ What's so great about a level playing field?

Nobel Prize–winning economist F. A. Hayek often wrote about the importance of free trade, once saying, "It is necessary in the first instance that the parties in the market should be free to sell and buy at any price at which they can find a partner to the transaction and that anybody should be free to produce, sell, and buy anything that may be produced or sold at all." The same conclusion is reached through the principle of comparative advantage—that free trade leads to the most efficient use of the world's resources and creates the greatest possible wealth for the greatest possible number of people.

Free trade allows people and businesses to specialize in what they have their greatest advantages in and trade the resulting goods and services for things they want and need that others have the advantage in producing. This way, prosperity increases as trading partners achieve better living standards than would have been possible in isolation.

But if all this is true, then why is there so much resistance to free trade? Has the world changed so much that we need a new theory to guide us?

Angling for a Bigger Piece of the Pie

In 1776, Adam Smith spoke in his book *The Wealth of Nations* about "the uniform, constant, and uninterrupted effort of every man to better his condition, the principle from which public and national, as well as private opulence is originally derived ...." In other words, we want to become wealthier and will go to great lengths to get there. The downside of free trade is that when consumers are free to purchase goods and services from distant places, merchants are faced with wider competition. It can be a hard enough thing to swallow when "elsewhere" is down the street or in a neighboring town, but what if "elsewhere" means that the product a potential customer chose over yours is made in a country thousands of miles away? Now the benefits of doing business not only bypasses our own pockets, but appears to leave the country altogether and profit outsiders.

Did You Know?

As Adam Smith told us long ago, all organizations and individuals have a profit motive, which means they want to be better off in the future than they are now, or were in the past. To that end, producers often push for measures that protect them from global trade but require others to pay higher prices.

Free-trade policies run into fierce resistance when businesses and workers lose income, jobs, and ways of life because competitive imported goods are selling better than their own, luring away customers and emptying the aisles of once-thriving enterprises. What can be done to stop the bleeding? Lots of things, but one popular alternative that is the subject of this chapter is to make those imported goods more expensive. Everybody knows that higher prices translate into lower sales, especially when a domestically produced alternative is available at a price that has suddenly become more attractive.

The Tariff Variations

A tariff is a tax that a country charges on particular goods when they cross its borders. Though sometimes taxes are charged on goods that are exported (leave the country), most tariffs are directed at imported goods (entering the country). For most American readers, export taxes sound strange, and for good reason: they are illegal. Because southern states once feared that northern states would impose export tariffs on cotton as a way to harm them through decreased revenues, they negotiated a stipulation in the Constitution that reads, "No tax or duty shall be laid on articles exported from any state."

There is no restriction on imposing tariffs on imported goods, and the United States has levied plenty of them, not unlike most other countries involved in global trade. Tariffs are charged on imported goods to protect producers from foreign competition or to raise money, and sometimes both at once.

Usually a tariff is not intended to completely eliminate an imported good (though you can be sure plenty of domestic producers hope they have exactly that effect); it is meant to put imports at a disadvantage when they cross national borders. At the same time, the domestic product has the advantage of a comparatively lower price than it used to have.

Specific Tariff

A specific tariff is a fixed sum of money charged for each unit of an imported good. When the products being charged this tax are standard items and easy to identify, a specific tariff is simple to administer. Such tariffs are also easy when the value of a particular good is difficult to determine or varies widely.

The disadvantage of a specific tariff is that its benefits diminish as the prices increase among a set of imported goods. For example, say your country protects the home-grown boat industry and charges a tariff of $2,000 for each foreign-made boat sold there. For a $15,000 boat, this makes a big difference; for a $200,000 boat, it does not. An unintended consequence could be that the homegrown industry feels compelled to focus on producing the cheaper boats. On the other hand, during hard economic times—when consumers look for bargains—this kind of tariff offers heightened protection.

Ad Valorem Tariff

In contrast to the set rate of a specific tariff, an Ad valorem tariff is a tax that is determined by a percent of a product's market value. For our previous boat example, a 20 percent Ad valorem tax on the $15,000 boat raises its price by $3,000 (to a total of $18,000), whereas a 20 percent tax on the $200,000 boat raises its price by $40,000 (to a total of $240,000). This kind of tariff does a more effective job of protecting the high end of a particular product range than the specific tariff can do.

In times of significant inflation (a rise in the overall price level), Ad valorem tariffs also have an advantage, for as prices rise, so do the collections from the tariff, and it does not have to be raised to play "catch up" with prices.

Of course, what seem like advantages to tax collectors may seem less like advantages to tax payers. This table shows a mix of imported goods and the U.S. tariffs on them. These tariffs include specific tariffs, Ad valorem tariffs, and combinations of the two:

Product	Tariff Imposed
Wrist watches	$.51 each
Fireworks	2.4% of value
Piano	4.7% of value
Electric motors	6.7% of value
Bicycles	5.5% of value
Umbrella	6.5% of value
Paprika	$.03/kg
Cotton blankets	8.4% of value

Source: United States International Trade Commission, 2007

Compound Tariff

What happens when a specific tariff and an Ad valorem tariff get together? Their off-spring is a compound tariff, which, depending on your perspective, combines the best or worst features of both. They are often used with manufactured goods when the goal is to protect both domestic producers of raw materials and those who sell finished goods. For example, if a country wants to protect its domestic mozzarella cheese industry while also shielding the makers of pizza from foreign pies, a compound tariff could be developed that looks similar to this: a $1 per pound levy on the mozzarella portion of the imported pizza plus 15 percent of the value of the finished pie.

The Effective Tariff Rate

The effective tariff rate is a measure of the actual level of protection a tariff provides for goods shielded from imports. It represents the difference between how much is produced with the tariff and how much would have been produced if free trade were allowed. Another way of looking at the effective rate is seeing how much more expensive a domestic good can be than the foreign competition and still be competitive in the market.

So how is the effective tariff rate different from the nominal (stated) tariff rate? A 30 percent import tariff on pants, for example, does not mean a country's pants industry is getting 30 percent worth of protection. The reason is that this import tariff is slapped on top of the final value of a pair of pants—what it is worth after it is done being made. During the production process, however, different materials or intermediate goods were used, with varying tariffs attached to them.

When Tariffs Breed More Tariffs

When tariffs are levied, they do not exist in isolation. These taxes change how economic markets function, bringing changes in prices, profitability, sales levels, revenues, expenses, market penetration, and expectations for the future. An exporter losing sales because a new tariff has been imposed will not just sit still and take it. A domestic producer reaping the benefits of tariffs will not watch those disappear without a fight. Producers push politicians to share their concern that other countries are "not playing fair" and lobby them to strike back.

In addition to all the above, tariffs can be significant sources of revenue for countries. Now that can be hard to pass up. Increasing inflows of cash simply by adding new taxes to goods made in other countries (where the citizens have no authority over the taxing government) is a real temptation. In 1900, before there was a federal income tax, 41 percent of the tax receipts collected by the U.S. government came from tariffs. Today, with federal spending much, much larger, income from tariffs is just 1 percent.

Most developing countries have populations whose average earnings per citizen are much lower than the wealthier developed countries. They also have less domestic industry to draw revenues from, so these factors make their tax collections seem surprisingly large. Wealthy countries impose tariffs on many of the goods produced in developing countries, which raises prices and thereby keeps export sales lower than would be possible within a free market system.

The Impact of Tariffs

The theory of the invisible hand claims that when the free exchange of a limited resource is allowed between individuals and organizations, the economy is guided to more efficient production. Markets mobilize information, and generate incentives to set efficient prices. When these prices are altered by outside forces, such as a new tax imposed by a government in the form of a tariff, the market is deprived of information and coordination, and will not do as well as it could have. When the visible hand of government officials, advised by domestic producers, reach into markets to fix tariff rates, they are rarely able to increase overall wealth.

Protecting the Producers

In an editorial for *The Wall Street Journal* in the mid-'80s, economist Milton Friedman told readers that the most patriotic thing they could do for the American auto industry was buy a Honda. At the time, the Big Three automakers (Ford, GM, and Chrysler) were pushing for restrictions on imported cars because, they claimed, American jobs and a huge American industry were at stake. From Friedman's perspective, protecting the U.S. auto industry by forcing higher prices on imported cars was not the answer. Yes, such measures would have protected some jobs in the auto industry and helped stem the erosion of market share to foreign competitors, but it would also interfere with a natural incentive for American companies to produce better cars: in a free market, inferior products lose out, so the choice is either to make better cars or allow business to be lost for good.

India, interestingly, took the protectionist route with automobiles, and for decades India's best-selling car, the Ambassador, looked like a British taxicab from the 1950s. Actually, the Ambassador *was* a British taxicab from the 1950s, copied from the British Morris Oxford, which produced British taxis. India finally liberalized its auto industry in the 1990s, allowing foreign car companies to import and build factories in India. Now Indian companies, such as Tata Motors, are responding by jumping into the market to produce world-class cars in India, and to export them to Africa and Latin America.

Until the end of the last century, India and East Germany set strict limits on the selling of automobiles made abroad. The intent was to protect domestically made cars and preserve jobs. Without the incentives provided by competitors beyond their borders, both countries were notorious for producing cars that were unreliable, uncomfortable, and decades out of date. In contrast to East Germany, West Germany, home of Mercedes and BMW, produced some of the best-loved and most profitable lines of automobiles in the world. Assuming that Germans in the pre-unification west were not inherently superior in car producing to their cousins in the east, it seems that the different attitude toward competition played a significant role.

To get back to Friedman, he stressed that protecting an industry shields jobs and sales, slows innovation, keeps prices artificially high, and does not allow consumers freedom to purchase products they find superior. The same argument holds in other sectors of the economy, too.

Do Consumers Foot the Bill?

It is consumers who ultimately bear the cost of tariffs and, by doing so, provide subsidies to the domestic industries being protected from foreign competition. In other words, paying a tariff is usually akin to contributing to a job's program—without being asked if you want to.

Why do we go along with this, especially those of us who are not interested in paying extra for somebody else to keep a job? For most goods with tariffs attached to them, the cost to individual consumers is not great enough to make complaining worthwhile. For example, the sugar industry benefits enormously from tariffs on imported sugar, but, according to the Institute for International Economics (based in Washington), all the millions that sweeten operations in that industry only amount to an average of $21 a year per American household. American-made luggage is another protected industry, but because a consumer only pays a few dollars more per suitcase and does not buy suitcases very often, why get worked up about it?

In short, the consumers who foot the bill for tariffs are spread out all over the country and rarely have to pay more than a small amount for particular protected goods. Organizing a dispersed group whose members are not losing a lot and trying to get them to take action is not an easy task. The beneficiaries of tariffs, in contrast, are clustered together as small groups who receive significant benefits, like workers receiving paychecks and owners making profits, so they have strong incentives to keep tariffs going.

Black Markets

Black markets exist when individuals buy and sell goods illegally. These goods might be illegal themselves, as in the case of opium, or can be legal goods that buyers and sellers seek to avoid paying taxes on. During Prohibition in the United States, alcohol production and consumption (of the sort people drink) was banned. Did that mean everybody quit drinking? Not a chance. Instead, enormous black markets, often run by criminal enterprises, developed where beer, wine, whiskey, and whatever else people want were manufactured and sold to consumers with thirsts soda could not quench.

Warning, Pothole Ahead!

In a black market, there is illegal economic activity going on, but this does not mean the economic good or service itself is illegal.

Similar kinds of markets arise for the trading of items not meeting domestic regulatory standards (certain medications) or whose prices are artificially high due to tariffs or restrictions on availability. Though there are negative consequences for being involved in black markets, from fines to prison, they continue to operate whenever the rewards of participating in the black market (satisfaction of drinking bourbon despite it being illegal) are perceived to exceed the combined dollar costs and risks.

The Exporter's Burden

How would you like to run a business where your products are priced higher than you want them to be, yet you do not get to keep any of the additional charge? On the contrary, the higher price means you receive less money than before, because your sales have dropped as consumers purchase cheaper alternatives. Such is the lot of exporters who have tariffs levied on their goods. In effect, the tariff is an additional cost of doing business that competitors in the country where it has been imposed do not have to pay.

Exporters faced with tariffs have a few choices. If there is still sufficient demand for their products even with the extra tax and they can make the profits necessary for the effort to be worthwhile, then why not stay? Less will be sold than could be if the tariff did not exist, but so be it. An exporter who is unable to compete as effectively as desired after the imposition of a tariff may simply decide to stop doing business in that country and focus on better opportunities.

The crux of the exporter's dilemma is that a tariff eats away at the very comparative advantage that makes trade desirable to begin with. It would come as no surprise to Adam Smith that, despite this, many an exporter who complains about tariffs imposed in other countries takes a very different view of them when they protect and insure profits on the home field.

Jobs Protected, Jobs Destroyed

Protecting jobs comes at a high cost. Jobs lost due to the higher costs that tariffs impose may be greater than jobs saved. Once again, those lost jobs are spread out and hard to quantify exactly, so we are not going to see people protesting about a job they hoped to get that has not been created because of tariffs.

Another difficulty, as we saw in the examples of the East German and Indian auto industries, is that industries protected by tariffs may suffer from a loss of incentive to be creative and competitive. So while Mercedes was spanning the globe establishing its brand name and growing sales revenue and employing an expanding workforce, its protected brethren in East Germany remained stagnant.

Just to provide a clearer idea of what tariff-financed jobs cost, let us continue with the sugar and luggage industry examples discussed previously. The $21 extra the average U.S. household pays for sugar translates into $826,000 that consumers pay for each job saved. In the luggage industry, 168,786 jobs have been saved. That is an impressive amount, but consider the cost: $200,000 paid in the form of higher prices for each of those jobs.

We know there is no such thing as a free lunch, and there is certainly no such thing as a tariff consumers don't have to pay.

The Least You Need to Know

- A tariff is a tax on imported goods intended to protect domestic producers and raise money.

- Consumers in the country imposing a tariff are the ones who bear the cost of it.

- The costs of tariffs are spread out but the benefits to industry owners and workers are concentrated.

- The cost to protect a job using a tariff is usually much higher than the pay received on that job.

Chapter 7

Manning the Barricades

In This Chapter

- Defining import quotas
- Carving up the market
- Subsidies and other financial aid for companies
- The practice of dumping

Efforts to take the bite out of foreign competition don't end with tariffs; there are plenty more where those came from! The goal remains the same, however: to protect domestic industries and jobs. Since World War II, the total number of restrictions has declined, but that doesn't mean they will continue falling. In a shrinking world where it gets harder and harder to keep "barbarians" from crossing the gates and cutting into domestic business, and where consumers usually choose according to their wallets, the urge to put up shields is natural and is not going away anytime soon.

Import Quotas: This Much and No More

From the cheese you eat to what you wear on your feet, there are, were, or might be restrictions on the amount that can be brought into the United States.

EconoTalk _____

A limit on the amount of a good that can be imported into a country during a specific period of time is an **import quota.**

Generally, the amount of a restricted good allowed past the borders is less than would come in under conditions of free trade. Because supply is limited, the price for the item is higher than it would be without an *import quota.* As with a tariff, consumers are forced to pay higher prices, which are intended to help domestic producers stay in business.

Who Pays, Who Profits?

The World Trade Organization outlawed quotas on imported manufactured goods a few years ago. Where they are used most often is in the shielding of domestic agricultural markets. Quotas are tough to administer, for not only do quota administrators have to decide how much of a foreign product is allowed in, they also have to decide who gets to bring in how much.

One approach is to set a total and then allow individual importers to apply for licenses allowing them to bring in a specific amount, with all licenses granted not exceeding the quota. Another method is to set quotas that stipulate how much of a particular product can come in from different countries. As you can imagine, there can be a lot of confusion as producers and importers scramble to bring in as much as possible before the ceiling is hit.

The following table is an example of import quotas set on milk and cheese coming into the United States from foreign countries.

Imported Good and Country of Origin	Annual Quota in kg
Condensed milk, Australia	91,625
Evaporated milk, Germany	9,887
Blue cheese, Argentina	2,000
Blue cheese, Chile	80,000
Cheddar cheese, New Zealand	8,200,000
Italian cheese, Poland	1,325,000
Italian cheese, Romania	500,000
Swiss cheese, Switzerland	1,850,000

Source: U.S. International Trade Commission

Assuming that more would be purchased if allowed to enter the country and prices would fall, American cheese producers are the beneficiaries. And who foots the bill? Foreign companies who lose out on potential sales and consumers who pay more when they buy cheese. Does it make sense to protect these products? That depends on whether the increased cost to consumers (which functions as a tax) is the best use of their money. Of course, if they thought so, they could send voluntary contributions to domestic cheese producers instead of being taxed. The question then becomes whether consumers should be allowed to buy however much they want of whatever they want, or if wiser heads need to direct them to better decisions.

Industries defending tariffs and quotas argue America should not have to rely on fickle foreigners for key goods and services. During the Reagan Administration, domestic shoe manufacturers argued that tariffs on imported shoes were a matter of national security and ran advertisements showing American troops marching off in socks to some future conflict. Steel manufacturers claim that restrictions on foreign steel are key to national defense. National defense claims regularly serve as trump cards in Congressional debates over trade restrictions.

How Different Are Tariffs and Quotas?

Tariffs and quotas are the two faces of industry shielding taxes. A tariff does its job by raising prices, but leaves quantities alone, which means it is still possible for a foreign good saddled with a tariff in the United States to be successful, so long as it is equal or superior to the domestic competition even after the extra charge has been tacked on. With quotas, on the other hand, there is a fixed amount allowed on the market that is not going to be increased, even if consumers are willing to pay more for it. What happens when customers want more of the good than allowed by quota? The price keeps going up until it hits the point where those willing to pay can purchase the good and those not willing to pay more forego the product.

One significant difference between tariffs and quotas is that tariffs generate revenue for the government from the higher prices consumers pay. Quotas, however, generate higher profits only for those lucky enough to have permits to import goods.

Tag-Teaming Trade

What happens when tariffs and quotas join forces? A double-barreled surcharge. In the United States this tag-team approach has been used on goods such as fish, sugar, milk, and steel.

This is how these two-headed monsters work: one tariff rate applies to a threshold amount of a particular good. When imports of it exceed the threshold, a higher tariff rate kicks in. This allows consumers to buy more than would be possible with a quota alone, but the tradeoff is that higher prices are charged for customers who really, really want this specific product.

In truth, when the next level tariff kicks in, it is a kick that lands with real force. Consumers are usually not required to pay just a little more, but are asked to fork over a penalty large enough to discourage all but the most wealthy and determined among them.

Permission to Enter

Since its founding in 1995, the World Trade Organization has been pushing for a move away from quotas and *tariff-rate quotas* to plain old simple tariffs. The advantage of these is that the costs are stated up front, and nobody has to worry about a ceiling being bumped into or a threshold crossed where goods suddenly take big jumps in price. Not only is the World Trade Organization promoting use of tariffs, they have been working to steadily decrease tariff rates themselves. So what are domestic industries to do when competitors show up on their shores? Call on alternative ways of slowing down their advance.

EconoTalk

The combination of a tariff with a quota has been dubbed the **tariff-rate quota.**

Divvying Up the Spoils

One approach is to carve up the market so that the competition for it is less intense: "You have your territory to run around in, but stay out of mine."

EconoTalk

When countries participating in trade devise an agreement mandating who gets to participate in what segment of the market, an **orderly marketing agreement** is born.

Orderly marketing agreements offer protection to domestic producers who might otherwise lose sales to foreign competitors offering better goods at lower prices. A nice break for the local guys, but again, consumers have to foot the bill. These agreements can also take the form of countries who dominate an industry coming to agreement on the total to be produced (as OPEC does). The purpose is to keep "excess" supply from driving prices down.

Marketing agreements are enacted less often today than in the past and their use has been restricted by trade negotiations in recent years. The expectation, then, is that these will fade away, but the temptation to protect domestic firms and influence markets remains, so we may see them mount a comeback in the future. Though no longer in force, the export quotas placed on Japanese automobiles entering the United States in the early 1980s gives us a good look at the effects. Most interesting is the tradeoff: an increase in American auto sales and jobs paired with greater costs to American consumers.

Estimated Impact of Japanese Export Quotas (1984)

Increased cost of Japanese autos:	$1,300
Increased cost of American autos:	$660
Cost to American consumers:	$15.7 million
Decrease in Japanese autos sold:	1 million
Decrease in Japanese share of market:	9.6%
Increase in American autos sold:	618,000
Increase in auto industry jobs:	44,000

Source: U.S. International Trade Commission, 1985

It is worth noting, too, that trade restrictions often have unintended consequences. Japanese automakers, limited by quotas to selling fewer cars in the United States, shifted to fancier cars that would earn high profits per car. Before the quotas, Japanese car imports were known as being small and cheap; as the quotas took effect, Japanese producers rolled out Lexus, Infinity, Acura, and other higher-priced models. As Japanese manufacturers captured market-share for the high-end cars, they hurt domestic car companies as much or more than they had with earlier inexpensive cars.

Ingredients the Recipe Cannot Rise Without

Instead of restricting how much of a foreign product can be imported, why not set standards for how much of a manufactured good must be assembled with parts that come from the home company? This removes the challenge of deciding on a limit and checking to make sure no one is making end runs around it. Identifying where component parts come from is easier to do.

Domestic content requirements are one way unions can try to battle feared job losses and pay cuts from foreign manufacturing. When these requirements are in force, the "hammer" to back them up is the threat of tariffs imposed on goods that do not meet the domestic content requirement. These can be directed at foreign-owned and native-owned companies alike.

Perhaps the best-known case of domestic content requirements has been in the automobile industry. In the United States, with market share falling steadily for the "Big Three" over the years, the protectionist goal was first to protect the American companies and then to have foreign manufacturers based in the United States use a minimum amount of parts made in America. Domestic content requirements do not have to be in place formally to work—the threat of one coming along is enough to convince companies to compromise to keep the boom from being lowered on them.

Following is a selection of countries and the percentages of domestic content they require in order for automobiles to avoid tariffs (which drive up the cost and make competition more difficult).

Country	Percentage
Argentina	76
Brazil	60
China	40
Colombia	30
Mexico	62
Uruguay	60
Venezuela	30

Source: Department of Commerce, 2004

Automobiles serve as an interesting illustration, because American law dictates that cars and trucks weighing less than 8,500 pounds have labels that tell consumers where the vehicle's parts came from. If you ever have the chance to check this out on auto lots, you might be surprised by the high percentage of American-made parts used by some manufacturers, like Subaru.

Keeping the Home Fires Burning

Another way to help out the home teams is to lower their costs with the goal of helping them to compete and sell more goods. This can be done by giving firms cash directly or taking indirect measures, such as loaning them money at low interest rates or providing things such as insurance at a lower price tag than could be found otherwise. Lowering various regulations and taxes would also assist domestic manufacturers in competing with foreign companies.

Paying the Producers

Though a *subsidy* does not directly raise the cost of a good for consumers, as tariffs and quotas do, they are not free. The money has to come from somewhere, and in this case that somewhere is tax dollars, so, you guessed it, consumers still pay—even if the route is less direct. Subsidies vary widely according to the level of government involvement in the economy, and the amount of influence different industries have on government policy (that's what they pay those lobbyists for).

EconoTalk

A **subsidy** is financial assistance the government provides to companies and specific sectors of the economy with the goal of promoting sales.

An **export subsidy** is provided to firms producing goods for export to other countries.

The following are a few examples of subsidies in play by different governments:

- **United States:** *Export subsidies* for agricultural and manufactured goods.

- **Canada:** Subsidies of railroad transportation costs for exporters of alfalfa, barley, oats, and wheat.

- **Japan:** Low-interest loans aid with research costs for producers of aerospace goods.

- **Australia:** Development grants for exporters that develop markets overseas.

- **European Union:** Money provided to Airbus; subsidies for agricultural products such as beef, poultry, fruits, dairy products, and wheat.

Disagreements over subsidies abound. To begin with, if one industry gets them, others wonder why they aren't also. Then there are cases of countries crying foul when domestic producers have to compete with goods they claim have unfair advantages via subsidies. For example, American lumber producers have long complained that prices of competing Canadian lumber are artificially low because the Canadian government provides them land at a cost below what would be paid on the open market.

Dumping for Dollars

What if you are in charge of export development for a country seeking to expand foreign markets and are in charge of developing strategies for it? Wouldn't it be tempting to help firms get their "feet in the door" by helping them charge less than the competition, and even less than they charge at home? The strategy has its appeal, and it has certainly been tried plenty of times, both at home and in foreign lands, but the practice has become increasingly controversial.

Price discrimination is the charge made when one group is charged a different price than another—so one person's bright strategy for market penetrations is another person's outrage at what is seen as an abusive practice. What if you, now the head of the Crooked Cookie Company, suddenly had to deal with cookies flooding the store shelves from abroad, where either the manufacturer, the country of origin, or both, are underwriting the costs of offering them at an artificially low price (for less than they cost to make, for example)? Sure, consumers would be thrilled at the cheap cookies, but now your sales are dwindling and you might have to lay off workers. For the Crooked Cookie Company, then, the deal is not so sweet.

Deals in the Dumps

Even though the practice of *dumping* can increase sales, does it really raise profitability? Remember, dumped goods are usually sold below the cost to make them, so it can be an expensive habit to maintain. If the goal is to drive competition from the market, however, the opportunity to raise prices in the future might be seen as a kind of light at the end of the tunnel. For consumers paying the lower prices, dumping is beneficial.

 EconoTalk

Dumping happens when less money is charged for a product sold abroad than is charged in the home country.

Shutting Down the Dump

Many countries have enacted laws to combat dumping, but it can be difficult to tell the difference between a competitor who is selling for less because of genuine efficiency and one who is simply trying to gain sales by selling at a loss.

Did You Know? _____

Sporadic dumping occurs when a competitor sells off excess inventory in another country for less than is charged at home.

Predatory dumping is the practice of temporarily lowering prices to drive a competitor out of business.

Persistent dumping is the continuous policy of selling a good for less abroad than is charged domestically.

In the United States, the Department of Commerce reviews *anti-dumping duties* and, as the criteria for deciding on the matter, tries to judge if the product is being sold below the cost of production. If Commerce decides it is, then the extra charge can be added to the price with the goal of bringing it up to a more realistic market value. Complaints made to the Department of Commerce also get filed with the International Trade Commission. Domestic producers file these complaints, but it turns out to be difficult to determine what actual costs of production are for overseas firms. In 2004, China slapped anti-dumping tariffs on cold-rolled steel from South Korea, Russia, Ukraine, and Kazakhstan. Chinese steel manufacturers were pleased, but how likely is it that the Chinese government had good data on steel production costs in other countries? In 2007, Ukraine's trade commission began an anti-dumping investigation of Chinese firms for dumping steel ropes and cable on Ukraine. And United States steel companies have filed complaints against both Chinese and Ukrainian firms for dumping steel products on U.S. markets.

EconoTalk _____

An **anti-dumping duty** is a charge levied on a good that is judged to be selling below its cost to produce.

There's More Than One Way to Skin a GATT

Since the inception of the General Agreement on Trade and Tariffs (GATT) there has been a push toward removing barriers to trade, be they tariffs, quotas, or dumping practices. Even if these barriers were banished forever (not likely, as the impulse to use them keeps cropping up), countries still find ways to maintain a "home field advantage."

Support Your Local Supplier

During the Great Depression in 1933, the federal government passed the Buy American Act. The act required federal agencies to buy from American suppliers so long as their prices were not "unreasonably" higher than those offered by foreign competitors. The American suppliers were themselves required to sell the government products whose domestic content was at least 50 percent.

In the years since the passage of the Buy American Act, the federal government has grown dramatically, as has the volume of its purchases. Though some of the act's provisions have been relaxed, it remains an important factor in federal purchases and many state and local governments have similar measures of their own in place.

The Least You Need to Know

- Quotas cause the prices of targeted goods to rise by restricting the supply of them.

- Quotas and tariffs make it easier for domestic companies to compete, but raise costs for consumers.

- Subsidies are direct forms of assistance given by governments to local companies, such as cash and low-interest loans.

- Dumping occurs when products made in one country are sold in a foreign country, or countries, for less than they cost to make.

Part 3

Knock Down the Old Gray Walls

In the United States, tariffs used to be the major source of federal government revenue; now, however, tariffs are efforts to protect domestic industry from overseas competition. Meanwhile, multinationals have made it harder to measure the transfer of goods and assets between branches in different countries. And do multinationals, with their "sweatshops" and transnational dealings, bring benefits to the developing world?

This part is a realistic examination of the kinds of things countries around the globe do to protect themselves from foreign competitors—while also trying to reap maximum benefits from the process themselves.

"He says he's got a McDonald's franchise inside."

Policies, Politics, and Global Regulators

In This Chapter

- Domestic industry tariffs
- General agreement on tariffs and trade
- GATT and the WTO

Tariffs today serve a different purpose than they did in the past. In the nineteenth century, as a growing United States economy looked for more markets abroad, tariffs were a way for the government to collect revenue. Though tariffs varied from good to even better, after the McKinley Law passed in 1890, the average tariff rate hit 48 percent. In contrast, in 2006 it stood at 4.4 percent. As you will see, there has been plenty of rising and falling in the years between. Of course domestic manufacturers in the 1890s were as happy to be protected from foreign competition as manufacturers are today. And as might be guessed by the high tariff rates, U.S. manufacturers were far less competitive and far more influential in lobbying for tariffs.

Manufacturers then could argue that tariffs both protected jobs and profits and provided significant revenue for the government. Now, however, tariffs only protect a particular industry or sector of the economy. Though the government collects money, it is not a significant portion of what it takes in. Since World War II, many countries around the world have been working together to reduce tariffs and other impediments to free trade—a worthy goal to be sure. But the way is bumpy, and suspicions abound that the light at the end of the tunnel is really a train—made by a foreign country. (Amtrak's high-speed Acela trains are made in Canada, by the way.)

Did You Know?

In 1913, the Sixteenth Amendment to the Constitution was ratified, giving the federal government the power to tax personal earnings. They started off small, with a tax of 1 percent on incomes of more than $3,000 and an additional 6 percent on incomes of more than $500,000. In 1918, the top tax rate rose to 77 percent on incomes of more than $1,000,000 and in 1945, a 45 percent tax rate was placed on incomes of more than $200,000. During World War II, payroll withholding was introduced to take federal taxes right out of paychecks. This was initially a temporary measure to help fund the war. It worked so well for reducing resistance to higher taxes that it became permanent after the war. In the following years, tariffs were gradually reduced as income tax rates and revenues increased.

A Taxing History

In 1791, the Secretary of the Treasury, Alexander Hamilton, wrote his *Report on Manufacturers* and presented it to Congress. In it, he made the connection between raising revenue for the country and benefiting domestic industries. At the time, the price increase imposed by a tariff was seen as purely beneficial, and there was little notion of burdening consumers with higher prices and losing out by not taking full advantage of comparative advantage (see Chapter 5 for more on comparative advantage).

Did You Know?

In 1791, Alexander Hamilton stated in his *Report on Manufacturers,* "… by enhancing the charges on foreign articles, they enable the national manufacturers to undersell all their foreign competition … it has the additional recommendation of being a resource of revenue."

Hamilton also made a case that has been repeated many times and in many places since: that developing industries should be protected from foreign competition until they can take root and make it on their own, otherwise known as an *infant industry argument*. In a new country struggling to establish itself, the appeal of this is obvious, just as it is to emerging economies in any time period.

EconoTalk

The **infant industry argument** is that new industries should be protected (in the form of tariffs, quotas, and other regulations) until they achieve an economy of scale that enables them to compete on an equal basis with foreign competitors.

Before the Axe Fell

Tariffs steadily rose in the early years of the nineteenth century. They peaked at an average of 45 percent in 1828 with what came to be known as The Tariff of Abominations for its high taxing on almost all foreign goods. After the War of 1812 there was a recession in Europe, and one of the results was a flood of low-priced goods from England that American manufacturers complained they couldn't compete with. The steadily increasing tariffs reduced the sales of British goods in America, but also had the unintended consequence of Britain retaliating by reducing their purchases of American cotton. This aggravated the southern states, who suffered the twin price shocks of higher prices for imported goods and a decrease in revenues from the sale of cotton and other agricultural products. Continuing on to the present, this has been a pattern seen over and over: a country seeks to guard an industry with protectionist measures, only to suffer the consequences of economic sanctions from affected nations.

In response to southern resistance, tariffs began heading back down in 1832. Just prior to the Civil War, tariffs were back to where they had been early in the century, around 16 percent. They rose again during the war as a means of financing the fighting (and because the war "reduced" resistance to tariffs from southern states). After the Civil War, tariffs continued to rise in response to pressure from American businesses that said they needed help to compete with foreign goods (sound familiar?).

What had gone up began coming back down in the early years of the twentieth century with a series of tariff reductions. By 1913, tariffs were down to an average of 27 percent. But then World War I came along and, you guessed it, tariffs climbed again. They continued their rise after the war in response to the now-usual complaint that it was too hard to compete with foreigners who had the advantage of lower costs.

The Smoot-Hawley Act

American tariff rates of the twentieth century peaked in 1930 with the Smoot-Hawley Act. It imposed a tax of 60 percent on a broad range of materials and products imported by the United States—3,200 of them. As had been seen a century earlier, foreign manufacturers hurt by the measure didn't just sit back and take it, they lobbied their governments to strike back.

Are Tariffs Depressing?

It used to be assumed that the Great Depression of the 1930s was caused by the failure of the market economy, which served as the justification for the New Deal measures that led to increased government intervention in the economy. Recent research has revised economists' views of the causes and especially the unprecedented length of the Great Depression. The one-two punch of increased tariffs and retaliatory trade restrictions by other countries led to both higher prices domestically and a decrease of exports. These trade disruptions added to a range of regulatory and monetary mistakes that not only threw the United States, but also much of the world, into a long, deep depression.

Did You Know? _____

One thousand economists signed a petition in opposition to the Smoot-Hawley Act, expressing their fear that other countries would strike back with their own tariffs. They were ignored, and the act passed—and the years that followed showed them to be right. America's primary trading partners—Canada, Britain, Germany, France, and many others—responded with a mix of their own new taxes on trade and a dramatic drop in exchange with the United States.

Imports declined from $4.4 billion in 1929 to $1.5 billion in 1933. From $5.4 billion in 1929, exports plunged to $2.1 billion. The unemployment rate stood at 9 percent in 1930, a high rate to be sure, and then leapt to 16 percent in 1931 and 25 percent in 1933. Not only did the American economy suffer, the rising tariff tide reduced Gross Domestic Product the world over. In the United States, the GDP fell 50 percent after passage of Smoot-Hawley.

Loosening the Reins

The fallout from Smoot-Hawley was a real-world example of what David Ricardo wrote early in the nineteenth century. For those who believed trade was a zero-sum game where the benefits went to winners who grabbed first and hardest, the years following widespread tariff escalation demonstrated the folly of that point of view. Ricardo claimed free trade increased the wealth available to the participants and that the benefits of trade were flexible and highest where markets function freely.

Making Rules to Play Nice By

Though tariffs and trade restrictions fell during the rest of the 1930s and into the 1940s, it wasn't until after the conclusion of World War II that this trend was formalized. It was initiated during the Bretton Woods Conference, which convened while the war was still being fought, in July of 1944. The overall purpose of the conference was to develop a strategy for economic recovery following the war's conclusion. An important part of this came in an approach for reducing the tariffs, quota, subsidies, and protectionist policies in general that had done so much harm. It was called the General Agreement on Tariffs and Trade (GATT); the agreement was outlined in 1944, fleshed out in 1947, and signed by 23 countries on January 1, 1948.

Countries Who Signed GATT on January 1, 1948

Australia	Cuba	Norway
Belgium	Czechoslovakia	Pakistan
Brazil	France	Rhodesia
Burma	India	Syria
Canada	Lebanon	South Africa
Ceylon	Luxembourg	United Kingdom
Chile	Netherlands	United States
China	New Zealand	

Getting Into GATT

GATT got off to a roaring start. The 23 countries involved made approximately 45,000 concessions on tariffs and other trade restrictions. These concessions affected more than $10 billion in global trade.

The first round of talks was followed by another held in France in 1949 that resulted in an additional 5,000 tariff reductions. More rounds followed in 1951, 1955–1956,

1960–1962, 1964–1967, and 1973–1979. The seventh round of the 1970s, held in Tokyo, showed how the agreement's scope was expanding. Not only were further tariff reductions achieved, steps were taken in the areas of import licensing, antidumping restrictions, subsidies, government procurement, and customs valuation. This trend continued in the next round of talks held from 1986–1993 in Uruguay. These proved to be the most ambitious to date. Not only was the expanded list from the 1970s picked back up, they also had serious discussions concerning agricultural products. In the past, this area had been "hands-off," but enough countries pushed to get it brought to the table that this sensitive area was examined, too.

> **Did You Know?**
>
> Though GATT was intended to become a formal organization, it never did. GATT remained an agreement designed to reduce barriers to trade between nations.

By this time, 125 countries were participating in the talks. Because GATT had never become an actual organization, there was widespread agreement that it was past time to have a formal organization devoted to the carrying out and expanding of the mission of GATT. And so the World Trade Organization was born.

What GATT Begat: The World Trade Organization

In 1994, the GATT members created the World Trade Organization (WTO) and promptly expanded the scope of the new institution (GATT ended at the conclusion of 1995). From the original mandate of GATT and the responsibilities it had added during the years, WTO delved into the service sector of the global economy and even tackled the thorny issue of intellectual property rights.

As membership grew and the scope of issues taken on widened, it was inevitable that disagreements would arise. Even though the WTO's mandate was to break down barriers and promote the benefits that follow from global trade, the interests of different countries often conflicted. When you think about it, this shouldn't be a surprise. Although international trade provides general benefits, it need not benefit those not party to the trade. Domestic manufacturers and farmers are happy to purchase lower-cost goods from overseas, but generally prefer their customers not have the same option.

> **Did You Know?**
>
> China became the 143rd member of the World Trade Organization in 2001.

And if competing interests within the WTO aren't enough, consider all the outside groups who have a stake in what the WTO does. An organization with so many members from all over the globe is sure to be a target of fear, suspicion, resentment, and plain old differences of opinion.

Did You Know?

Delegates to the December 1999 WTO summit held in Seattle found streets clogged with crowds of well-organized protestors, many determined to disrupt the talks. The talks were already salted through with controversy, with conflicts brewing about labor standards, intellectual property, the environment, and agricultural subsidies. Protestors shared these concerns, along with fears of corporate domination, damage to the environment, the exploitation of Third World workers, and government and corporate control of the media, the global economy, and the WTO itself.

Eventually the talks got underway, but the dissension in the streets was reflected in the meetings, and little agreement or progress was made.

Trying to Throw the Weight of the World Around

The WTO has a process for resolving disputes, and it is one that has seen a lot of business. All WTO members are supposed to be committed to open markets for trade between nations, and most surely are. The disagreements usually come down to fair trade versus unfair trade. What we hear is often the stated desire to use the process to create a level playing field. The problem is that one nation's level playing field is another's slippery slope. As we saw in earlier chapters, each country has a unique set of resource endowments. In fact, if there really was a level playing field and everybody was on par with everybody else, much of the reason for trade would disappear.

 **Warning, Pothole Ahead!**

It is because people, companies, cultures, and climates are unequal in their resources, talents, policies, and institutions that trade is so beneficial. Each can specialize in their areas of strength, and if these areas are smoothed out, the benefits of economic globalization decline.

A condition of WTO membership is that member countries allow the WTO to resolve trade disputes rather than take action themselves. In reality, countries do take action on their own, but the WTO's mechanism keeps down the level of friction.

Steps in the WTO Dispute Resolution Process

1. Consultation and mediation. When a country files a complaint against another, they are directed to first attempt resolving the issue themselves, with the WTO available to assist in negotiation. Time period: 60 days.

2. Panel is put together. If the consultation and mediation fail to resolve the dispute, an independent panel is assembled to investigate the issue and advise the WTO. Time period: three to six months.

3. The panel provides a report on its findings and recommendations to the countries involved. Three weeks later the same report is submitted to the WTO.

4. The WTO accepts or rejects the report. Time period: 60 days.

Source: World Trade Organization

If the WTO's decision is appealed and an appeals panel considers it, they have 60 to 90 days to issue a report. The WTO then has 30 days to accept or reject it.

If a country is found by the WTO to be in violation of a rule, the country is given time to outline how it will comply and is given approximately 3 to 15 months to make the changes. If they do not follow through on compliance, sanctions can be imposed on them, usually as fines, until they make the necessary changes.

Going into the Later Rounds

Though it is easy to question the accomplishments of the WTO, it should be kept in mind that it is a larger undertaking than the original GATT and addresses issues where GATT feared to tread. Though the gains from dramatically increased global trade have raised living standards across most of the world, the basics of economics still apply: there is never enough of the goods and services people want. And as present wants are satisfied, new wants arise. This is a constant that no organization can change.

Doha Opens Up a New Century

The latest of the WTO talks is the Doha Round and was launched in Doha, Qatar, in November 2001. The primary emphasis has been to include more countries in the economic globalization process and to help the poor in developing countries. In terms of trade, this can be promoted by eliminating tariffs on goods produced and exported by developing countries, and by getting rid of the subsidies rich countries give their agricultural sectors so that agricultural exports of poorer countries have a better chance of competing effectively.

A snag here is that although poor and emerging economies would benefit from the lowering agricultural trade barriers and subsidies, agricultural interests in developed countries would not benefit, at least in the short run. Even though the actual dollar amounts may be a small percent of total business done, special interests tend to be very focused on the trade barriers that protect their jobs and businesses.

Getting on the Fast Track

As we will see in the chapters ahead, the WTO is not the only game in town. Countries enter into their own trade agreements or associations. In the United States, one form in particular has been successful at promoting, on a smaller scale, the kinds of advantages sought after by the GATT in the past and the WTO today.

In 1974, Trade Promotion Authority, nicknamed "fast-track authority," was devised to give the president of the United States authority to institute trade negotiations with another country. When the president notifies Congress that he is taking this action, they have 60 days to approve or disapprove the fast-track negotiations. If approved, the president moves forward with the process and tries to hammer out an agreement. If one is made, it is presented to Congress for a vote that has to be made within 90 days.

In addition to the accelerated time frame, the other advantage of fast-track authority is that it eliminates the burden of congressional amendments, both in the negotiations themselves and when the vote is taken. With all the vested interested involved, you can imagine the provisions that could easily weigh down any agreement.

A major debate among economists, though, is the tradeoff between bilateral or multilateral trade agreements, in which two or more countries agree to reduce trade barriers between them; and worldwide trade agreements that GATT and now the WTO focus on. The fear is that trading blocks might reduce trade barriers among themselves but erect higher barriers against countries in other trading blocks.

Doing It with Duties

As with the WTO, fast-track agreements come with clauses that dictate what can be done if the agreement's terms are violated. The violations guarded against include things such as dumping, subsidizing products, abusive labor practices and, in general, anything that impairs free trade.

When violations are found, they are usually first addressed in meetings with the country found to have been breaking the rules. If the problem is not resolved, the next step is sanctions. These sanctions usually involve levying duties, which are similar to fines or tariffs, so that the offending country is charged for the continuation of the offense. An advantage of bi-lateral fast-track agreements is that disputes do not go before an international body. This gives a country more control over the process and, knowing that mechanism is there, can actually help agreements get passed.

The Least You Need to Know

♦ The restrictions on trade today are much less than they were in the nineteenth and twentieth centuries.

♦ No matter how effectively fair trade is promoted, conflicts will arise because resources are limited and it is impossible to satisfy all wants.

♦ Fast-track agreements are a means of promoting improved trade relations on a smaller scale than the WTO.

♦ Because countries have different sets of resources, talents, traditions, and policies, level playing fields for trade are hard to define.

Chapter 9

Up-and-Coming Economies

In This Chapter

- The balance of payments
- A breakdown of buyer and seller benefits in transactions
- National debit and credit records
- Is the United States in economic trouble?

Americans are used to thinking of their country as the 800-pound gorilla among the world's economies. In many ways it still is, but a look at economic data tells us that the United States is not as overwhelmingly dominant as it was just a couple decades ago.

For many years, the United States was the world's leading exporter, but this changed in 2006, when Germany edged ahead in this category. Not only that, but in the last six months of 2006, China exported more than the United States. Even more surprising, perhaps, is that more cars were made in China than the United States in 2006. And speaking of cars, Toyota is closing in on General Motors as the biggest auto manufacturer on the planet (and may have taken the lead by the time you read this).

It is not just by a few measures here and there that other countries are catching up and passing the United States. Goldman Sachs has predicted that China's economy will produce more than America's by 2027. When considered in terms of purchasing power (a comparison made based on how much can be purchased with respective currencies within their own borders), China could take the lead as early as 2011.

Does this mean that America's day is done? By no means. Today, California still produces more than all of China. Given its huge population and rapid rate of economic growth, China's growing presence in the global economy should not be a surprise. In some ways, China is simply returning to a position it held in the past; between the sixteenth and early nineteenth centuries, China led all western countries in farming techniques, sported bigger cities, and had better-educated citizenry.

In this chapter, we look at how to quantify the performance of economies, which allows us to compare them in the past and present, and make projections for the future. It's fine to talk about all the changes in the global economy and who are up-and-comers, down-and-outs, or just-holding-steadies, but we need an objective way to measure and compare performance. As you'll see, these methods aren't perfect and don't account for everything, but they are a worthwhile means of measuring and do tell us quite a bit.

Opening the Books

Economists use two sets of tools to measure the productivity of nations and their transactions with each other: national income and balance of payments accounting. For those of you who have taken accounting in the past and thought you had left it behind for good, you are about to be reacquainted—on a larger scale.

And just for good measure, you'll see the balance of payments again when we learn about money and how nations around the globe use it to exchange resources with each other.

You Say GNP, I Say GDP

We know that GDP is the value of all final goods and services produced within a country's borders during a specific year. A similar measure is GNP (Gross National Product), the value of all final goods and services produced and sold by a country's factors of production during a specific year. The difference between the two is that the GDP count occurs within a nation's borders, no matter who is doing the producing. GNP counts a country's production, no matter where it is produced. So, for example, GNP would count all BMWs made in America as a good produced by Germany, because that is where the company is owned. GDP counts it as American because that's where those particular BMWs are made. A German citizen providing services in the United States would see them counted in America's GDP, but his home country regards it as part of their GNP. Got it?

In reality, the differences between GDP and GNP are relatively small. Today, GDP is used far more often in economic statistics than GNP is. When we look into accounting for the incomes of nations, however, GNP is more accurate, so we will use it in this chapter.

Warning, Pothole Ahead!

Though GDP, GNP, and the income measures discussed in the following sections are valuable, they do not take into account things such as quality of life, the health of the environment, or human happiness. In other words, they are not the last word on a nation's well-being.

Paying the Producers

A country's GNP must always equal its income. Why? Think of it this way: every dollar spent on goods and services is income to some person or firm. If you pay $200 for a dentist to whiten your teeth, that is income to her. If you spend $25,000 on a new Ford, that is income for Ford.

Keeping the Right Count

It's not as complicated as it sounds if you remember that GNP is the final value of goods and services. A loaf of bread produced by a baker is counted in GDP, but the intermediate steps, such as acquiring the flour and yeast that go into it, are not. This is done to avoid double counting. We don't have to worry about all the money that changes hands on the way to the final loaf, just what it is sold for—if it is sold for $2, then that $2 is added to GNP and counted as income.

A Penny Earned Is a Penny Spent

Every transaction is both spending for the buyer and earnings for the seller. The seller spends money to purchase the ingredients and pays for labor and other factors of production—all this spending is income for others.

All Used Up and Nowhere to Go

In most countries with national accounting systems, consumption is the largest portion of GNP. Consumers buy what their countries produce in the form of toasters, cars, DVDs, food, and a long list of other things. In the United States, about two thirds of GNP goes to consumption annually.

Financing the Future

A good way to look at investment spending is as the part of GNP that is devoted to producing more goods and services in the future by increasing a nation's stock of capital.

> **EconoTalk**
>
> **Investment** is the portion of a country's current output that private firms use for future output.

Girders and sheet metal used to construct buildings are *investments*, as are the services of the architect who designed the buildings. When a company buys inventory, as in a shoe store adding more shoes to their selection, that is also considered investment. The reason is that buying inventory today for sale in the future transfers production from use in the present to use in the future (when it is sold). Unlike consumption spending, investment varies considerably. In the United States, it has ranged from 12 percent to 22 percent during the last two decades.

> **Warning, Pothole Ahead!**
>
> It is easy to confuse the kinds of investment you as an individual make with what economists consider to be a country's investment. The stocks and bonds you buy do not qualify as goods or services when GNP and GDP are calculated.

Our Tax Dollars at Work

Since the late 1950s, the American government has purchased about 19 percent of GNP each year. These government purchases encompass things such as spending on education, the armed forces, roads, and medical research. Money the government spends on things such as Medicaid, Social Security, and unemployment benefits are not considered government purchases, because the government does not receive any goods or services in exchange for the spending.

The Current Account

In a global economy, not all GNP has to be consumed, purchased, or invested at home. It can be sold to other countries, just as a portion of another country's GNP can be purchased. What we buy from another country (imports) is income to them; what we sell to another country is income for us.

It would be very unusual for exports and imports to come to the same number. In national accounting systems, imports are subtracted from exports. If exports are greater than imports, the difference is called a *current account* surplus. If exports are less than imports, the difference is called a current account deficit.

EconoTalk

The **current account** keeps track of the goods and services sold by countries and those that are sold to them by other countries.

Putting It All Together

Now that we've discussed where GNP goes, we can put all the accounts together. Not only do we know that Gross National Product equals Income, we also know that …

Consumption + Investment + Government Purchases + Exports – Imports = Gross National Product

The following table provides an example of how the equation works in a simple, fictional economy. Fish Island's entire GNP consists of fish burgers. The citizens of Fish Island eat 210 burgers, 75 are invested in the cultivation of future fish burgers, 30 are purchased by the government and used to build roads and homes, and 40 fish burgers are sold to Mango Island. Because all this fishy business makes the citizens of Fish Island thirsty, they buy 30 gallons of mango juice, which is equal in value to 55 fish burgers.

National Income Accounts for Fish Island

Gross National Product	300 fish burgers
Fish burgers consumed	210
Fish burgers invested	75
Fish burgers purchased by government	30
Fish burgers exported	40
Mango juice imported	(55)
Total	**300**

Incomes are rising around the world, and most people are better off than in the past, but measures of income, consumption, and investments do not capture the full extent of the advances made in the quality of life (how do you measure dentistry that is more expensive yet far less painful?). The United States, Japan, and Germany have continued to advance, but in recent years, increasing numbers of people in developing countries are also growing wealthier.

Consider some of the following gains made in American life between 1900 and 2000:

1. The average harvest per farmer in 2000 was 100 times what it was in 1900.

2. In 1900, 1 of every 10 babies died at birth; today's mortality rate is 1 in 150.

3. The average American enjoys a higher standard of living today (housing, transportation, entertainment, quality of food) than the richest American could have in 1900.

4. Leisure time increased about 300 percent from 1900 to 2000. The average American workweek in 1900 was 55 to 60 hours.

5. Most teenagers worked in agriculture or factories in 1900. In 2000, most were in school.

6. In 1900, the average life expectancy was 47 years. By 2000, it hit 77 years.

Source: http://eh.net/encyclopedia/article/whaples.work.hours.us

Debits and Credits and Deficits, Oh My!

Businesses keep track of the resources flowing in and out. Using dollars as a unit of measure, they record what they earn (revenues), what they spend to generate those earnings (expenses), what they own (assets), what they owe (liabilities), and their net worth (equity). It's a little different for countries, because they themselves are not for-profit entities.

Did You Know? _____

Think of a debit in the balance of payments as being similar to an expense in a business accounting system—an entry that reflects an outflow of resources. Credits are similar to revenue entries; they record resources flowing in.

Countries use balance of payment accounts to record the money they receive from foreigners and the money they pay to foreigners. Whenever a payment is made to a foreigner, it is recorded as a debit. Payments received from foreigners are recorded as credits. These events, essentially bookkeeping entries, are recorded and compiled by government statisticians and economists.

The Equation of Equations

When a debit is recorded in a nation's balance of payments account, a credit is also recorded. Not only that, total debits and total credits must equal the same sum. The accounting equation used in the balance of payments is self-balancing, also a feature of business accounting systems.

Did You Know? _____

Double-entry bookkeeping was first described in print by Luca Pacioli in 1494 (although it was in existence before then). Though today's accounting systems are more complex, the basics remain the same.

Three kinds of global transactions are entered into the balance of payments. They, and where they get recorded, are described in the following sections.

Current Events

When goods and services are exported or imported, they are recorded at their dollar value (or whatever currency a country works) in the current account. If you buy bratwurst from Germany, the German current account is credited for the purchase. At the same time, the American current account is debited.

Financial Assets

If financial assets are bought and sold between countries, the transactions are entered into the financial account. A financial asset is a mechanism for holding wealth and can take the form of stocks, bonds, money, or property. If you buy a Spanish stock, the transaction is recorded as a debit in the United States' balance of payments (outflow of money) and as a credit in Spain's (inflow of money).

A Capital Matter

Some other flows of wealth between countries are entered into the capital account. For the United States, these are small amounts that reflect mostly nonmarket activities such as debt forgiveness, some intangible assets (such as patents and copyrights), or immigrants bringing assets into the country.

It All Adds Up in the End

A confusing aspect of the balance of accounts is that the individual accounts all have credit or debit balances. How is that possible if total debits must always equal total credits? Even though this is true for every transaction and the system as a whole, a balanced entry will have debits and credits going to different accounts. Therefore, we can have individual accounts with greater or lesser debit and credit totals, but when added up, the final number is in balance.

An example of a system in balance is shown in the following table, in the United States' balance of payments. Note that the current account has a $530.7 billion debit balance, which means the United States bought more goods and services from foreigners than they bought from Americans. At the same time, however, those foreigners invested more in the United States than the United States invested in them, which translates into a $545.80 credit balance.

2004 United States Balance of Payments (in Billions)

	Credits	Debits
Current Account		
Exports		
Goods	713.1	
Services	307.4	
Income received	<u>294.4</u>	
Total exports	1,314.9	
Imports		
Goods		1,260.7
Services		256.3
Income payments		<u>261.1</u>
Total imports		1,778.1
Net unilateral current transfers	67.4	
Current account balance	530.7	
Capital Account	3.1	
Financial Account		
U.S. Assets Held Abroad		
Official reserve assets	1.5	
Other assets		<u>284.9</u>
Total U.S. assets held abroad		283.4
Foreign Assets Held in U.S.		
Official reserve assets	248.6	
Other assets	<u>580.6</u>	
Financial account balance	545.8	
Statistical discrepancy		12.0

Source: United States Department of Commerce

Half Full or Half Empty and Leaking?

There is considerable disagreement about whether the growing current account deficits represent an impending crisis for the United States or if it really isn't a big deal—or maybe even a sign of health. That's a pretty broad range of opinion, and it's based on the same sets of facts and figures.

The Scorekeeper Strikes

If we look at the current account as a running scorecard that tells us how well or poorly the United States is competing with other countries, we'll probably be discouraged by the results. Isn't it bad if they sell more to us (score more points) than we sell to them? Look at it this way: you probably have a deficit with a local fast-food restaurant, which means that you buy more from them than they buy from you. Is that bad? Only if you are not getting your money's worth. If you view the food as a good deal, then you are probably better off for having bought it.

The point here is that what really matters is value for the money, and opinions can vary widely on that. If Americans buy so much from foreigners, it must be because the same products at the same price and quality are not made available by domestic producers. In that sense, then, individual consumers are making efficient decisions by buying from beyond their borders.

Living Beyond Our Means?

If we buy more than we produce (GNP) and production equals income, then we are spending more than we have earned. That can only be done by borrowing. The funds for borrowing come to us through the investments other countries make in the United States. The worry, then, is that this borrowing, plus interest, has to be repaid eventually. As with any kind of borrowing, its ultimate value comes in what we do with it. Investment funds flowing into the United States do not just finance buying foreign chocolate and televisions, they also get directed toward things that create new jobs and foster economic growth.

At present, foreign countries own more than $2.5 trillion of American assets. That is a huge sum, but bear in mind that the United States has the largest, most powerful, most diverse, most stable, and most wealthy economy on the planet. Put in perspective, that number isn't as large as it looks.

Does It All Come out in the Wash?

Even if foreign investors decide America has overextended itself and isn't as attractive a place to invest in as it once was, disaster does not have to follow. The reason is that the value of the dollar will adjust to reflect the change, and the United States could eventually have a current account surplus instead of a deficit. How does that work? All shall be made clear in the chapters on money and exchange rates, so read on!

The Least You Need to Know

- Historically speaking, there is nothing unusual about economies rising or falling in prominence over time.

- The final value of the goods and services produced by a country is the same as its total income.

- Nations use double-entry accounting systems to keep track of transactions with other nations just as businesses use double-entry accounting systems to track exchanges with customers and other businesses.

- Surpluses and deficits in the current account are neither good nor bad by themselves. It is how wisely spending is done that matters most.

10

Will Multinationals Eat the World?

In This Chapter

- ◆ The rise of multinationals in developing countries
- ◆ Moving business to a foreign country
- ◆ Wage wars and the sweatshop controversy

A common stereotype of multinational firms portrays them as behemoths venturing forth from rich countries such as the United States, England, Japan, and Germany with the mission of swallowing up all that lies before them, including each other. They are viewed as having no loyalty to nations or workers at home as they seek cheaper labor abroad in the quest to produce more, sell more, and profit more in every corner of the globe.

Sure, multinational companies want to contain costs and make profits, but in a rapidly changing world they, too, are changing. Though they have been around since the twelfth century, what you see today is not your father's multinational. Many of today's players won't be around in a few years, while others will emerge. The hope for consumers is that, wherever they live, they will benefit from the process.

The Evolution of Multinationals

Though the process of globalization has opened up new markets to the traditional *multinational* firms, it has also provided opportunities for hungry, aggressive new firms springing up in the developing world. In the first three months of 2007, Indian firms spent $10.7 billion acquiring 34 foreign companies. In the same time period, Russian companies spent $11.4 billion buying foreign enterprises. Not long ago, venerable IBM sold its personal computer operation to Lenovo, a Chinese company.

EconoTalk

A **multinational** operates across national borders and may be owned and directed by individuals in various countries.

New firms in China, India, South Korea, and other countries pose serious challenges to the established multinationals, just as Toyota did in the auto industry not long ago. The new multinationals are fast and flexible, without the weight of heavy management structures or slow decision-making processes. Not only that, but, in a trend that goes against the "brain drain" phenomena we've all heard about, the old guard multinationals find themselves losing local employees to homegrown competitors that offer them more appealing career paths.

Your People or Mine?

As companies go global, the trend is to operate wherever the best combination of resources, markets, and business environments exist. For example, IBM employs more than 53,000 people in India and plans to hire more, making India their largest site outside the United States.

In the nineteenth century, expanding companies began from their home base and set up smaller versions of their operations in other countries, with the decision-making power remaining at home. The emerging model is to set up where the opportunities are best and make that the place where decisions are made. Instead of an old-fashioned multilevel company with a clear chain of command whose highest levels stay put, we will see more firms with related components roughly on par with each other.

Not So Fast

Though we have emphasized the changes in multinationals, there is still much that remains the same. Established multinationals flexible enough to adapt to a changing world still have significant advantages. Established firms draw upon a storehouse of knowledge and expertise, and those that have survived over time have developed skills to adapt to and prosper from new opportunities. Following is a list of the world's 10 largest corporations in 2006. Note how many are headquartered in the United States—though things can always change, having 6 out of 10 is not bad.

World's 10 Largest Corporations in 2006 (in Billions of Dollars)

Company	Headquarters	Revenues	Profits
Exxon	United States	334.0	25.3
Wal-Mart	United States	315.7	11.2
Royal Dutch Shell	Netherlands	306.7	25.3
BP	United Kingdom	297.6	22.3
General Motors	United States	192.6	–10.6
Chevron	United States	189.5	14.0
DaimlerChrysler	Germany	186.1	3.5
Toyota	Japan	186.0	12.1
Ford	United States	177.7	2.0
ConocoPhillips	United States	166.7	13.5

Source: The Global 500, Fortune

There's More Than One Way to Diversify

Given the changes in how even established companies operate, there is no standard for how multinational firms are organized. Here we'll take a little time to cover the major categories, but keep in mind that these borders, too, are blurring.

1. **Vertical organization:** This occurs when companies perform steps in the production process at different places, such as extracting oil on the way to making gasoline and plastic or making steel that is later shaped into final goods.

2. **Horizontal organization:** In this case, a company making a product in one location begins making the same thing in another country. This could include anything from jeans to soft drinks to cars.

3. **Conglomerate organization:** Sometimes multinationals are called conglomerates. Conglomerates are multinationals that have expanded into different lines of business from where they started.

Multinationals also expand their capacities by acquiring command of foreign companies by investing enough to gain a controlling interest. As demonstrated in the following table, countries direct most of their foreign investment into countries they have significant things in common with.

Though this, too, will change over time, it is interesting to note how much of a nation's investment in other countries goes to places that are similar, be it in standard of living or culture. Case in point: the following is a list of how much the United States invested in other countries and areas of the world, and how much those countries and areas invested in the United States in 2004 (in billions):

Country	Investment In ($)	Investment From ($)
Canada	216.6	105.3
Europe	1,090.0	100.1
Latin America	325.9	69.6
Africa	22.3	2.2
Middle East	19.2	7.9
Asia	390.1	192.6
Total	2,064.0	1,278.0

Source: U.S. Department of Commerce

Why Invest Beyond the Borders?

Not only do foreign operations boost the revenues of companies who are pushing against the market limits at home, investment from abroad can be a real boon, creating new jobs, spreading new technology, and generating economic growth. Multinationals invest where they see the greatest profit potential. When a company develops competitive skills and technologies and succeeds in home markets, it makes sense for them to try to duplicate that success in foreign markets.

Digging for Demand

Before a multinational opens for business in a foreign country, they must see a strong existing or potential demand there. Maybe they already export goods to the country and view setting up a base of operations there as a good way to develop the market further. Maybe the opportunity to draw on local talent will enable the firm to better fit its wares to the local market.

Did You Know? _____

> The first car Subaru manufactured was the Subaru 360 in 1958. It was made and available only in Japan. As the first auto manufacturer to make all-wheel-drive cars that were reliable and moderately priced, they saw great potential in the American market, particularly in the snowy northern states. They therefore opened a Subaru manufacturing plant in Lafayette, Indiana, in 1988. In 2006, Subaru America reported their best sales year ever, with 200,703 vehicles sold in North America.

Moving In on the Competition

A multinational might decide to operate in another country as a means of keeping a competitor who is already there from locking up the market. Let's say you are worried that your thriving bagel business will have an awfully hard time cracking a particular foreign market if you wait while a competitor keeps growing there. Instead of taking the time to build a new facility there, you could acquire an existing plant and invest the time and money in preparing it to pump out your product.

Counting the Costs

There are a lot of costs to consider when doing business in another country. One attraction of setting up shop in a less developed country is that the labor, materials, and regulatory costs may be significantly less than they are at home. When a solid cost advantage exists, a multinational may go much further than simply producing products for the local economy; they can also use the location as a base from which to export to other nations—or even back home.

If we go back to bagels to illustrate, say you want to find a good spot where your bagels can be made, frozen, and shipped to hungry consumers around the world. A place that features low materials and labor costs is going to be attractive, as will one where the cost to operate the enterprise (energy, and so on) is reasonable and transportation systems are good. Weather can be important, too. What if you want a climate friendly to growing your own wheat, or one good for cows so that you can make and market premium cream cheese to go with those bagels?

Who's in Charge There?

Governments have a lot to do with decisions multinationals make about where to set up shop, sometimes in ways you wouldn't expect. Back in the 1980s, American auto manufacturers clamored for restrictions on the Japanese imports that were cutting into their markets. It is interesting to note that during and after this time, a number of Japanese and German auto firms built factories in the United States. Things such as availability of labor, parts, geography, facilities, tax policies, and others surely influenced them, but avoiding tariffs and quotas by producing cars in America rather than exporting them probably had a lot to do with the trend. And American multinationals have pursued the same strategy by setting up operations in other countries rather than facing restrictions on their products entering those countries.

Political stability is also important, especially when it concerns property rights. What multinational is going to open up a new facility in a country they fear might become hostile to business in general, or their business in particular?

Did You Know?

On January 9, 2007, prior to being sworn in for another term, Hugo Chavez, the president of Venezuela, announced that some energy and telecom companies operating in his country were going to be nationalized. In response, Venezuela's stock market dropped by 10 percent. This drop was also fueled by Chavez expressing the desire to strip Venezuela's central bank of its independence and his call for a constitutional amendment allowing him greater power to rule by presidential decree. After swearing in his new cabinet, Chavez was quoted as saying, "We're heading toward socialism and nothing and no one can prevent it."

A License to Fill

Multinationals are not limited to choices of building or buying facilities in foreign countries if they cannot serve the market solely by exporting. One alternative, used by beer manufacturers, for example, is to license the production and sale of goods in other countries. This eliminates the need for new building and extensive buying, though they do need to share the profits.

Another alternative is to go into business with a foreign company or group of companies. A *joint venture* provides the opportunity for each party to contribute their expertise with the goal of operating more effectively than would be possible if one

firm went it alone. These ventures can include two or more firms and are very flexible
in terms of ownership interests, duties,
chains of command, and how the return on
investment is allocated.

> **EconoTalk**
>
> A **joint venture** is a partner-
> ship where each firm con-
> tributes resources and shares in
> the risks and profits.

Exploiting or Uplifting?

When multinationals pursue low costs and high profits, controversy can follow. Are
they gaining wealth at the expense of those kept in poverty? Should they be forced
to share more of that wealth? Or should they just be left alone to compete, provided
they obey the law? Are they "bending" laws in developing countries by influenc-
ing government officials? Part of the confusion stems from questions of justice and
profits. Do profits result from employees working harder, sharper management, more
sophisticated machinery, good luck, or some mysterious combination? Is there such a
thing as "fair" wages or "just" prices?

One Man's Fortune Is Another Man's Pittance

The ongoing sweatshop controversy is a good example of where wages paid by multinationals are often viewed as exploitative and far below what the workers should
be paid. Remember the scandal a few years ago that arose when it was revealed
that Kathy Lee Gifford's clothing line relied on low-paid workers in Honduras?
By American standards, the pay was atrocious, but what about the standards there?
Remember, the economic way of looking at things takes into account opportunity
costs, the value of the next best opportunity. If the next best opportunity of a worker
in a clothing factory is a job with even longer hours, lower pay, and worse conditions
(or perhaps no job at all), are they being exploited?

> **Did You Know?**
>
> In the Spring 2006 issue of *Journal of Labor Research,* Benjamin Powell published
> the results of a study called *Third World Living Standards: Are the Jobs Worth the
> Sweat?* He looked at the apparel industry in 10 Asian and Latin American countries and
> examined 43 complaints of unfair wages in 11 countries. It turned out that the so-called
> sweatshops paid workers better than the local alternative employment, and at rates sig-
> nificantly better than average. In the countries studied, 75 percent of the population was
> living on less than $2 a day, yet a 10-hour day in the apparel industry yielded much
> more. For example, in Honduras apparel workers earned $13.10 per day on average,
> whereas 44 percent of the country lived on less than $2 a day.

Minding the Managers

Multinationals vary widely in the kinds of jobs they offer to local workers. A company in a labor-intensive industry that builds a new factory is going to employ lots more people than one that buys an existing firm and doesn't expand its operations.

Management varies widely as well. Do the multinationals bring in their own people to run things, or do they hire or train citizens of the country to assume leadership roles? General Electric continues to train and send out its own managers to different countries. IBM, heading in another direction, is increasingly likely to use managers who are citizens of the nations they do business in.

Sharing Know-How

Not only do countries benefit from the new jobs provided by multinationals and the increased spending that promotes economic growth, they also benefit from the spread of new knowledge and skills through their population.

Knowledge comes not just in the form of a body of facts, but in ways of doing things, which includes everything from making tangible products to managerial techniques for the efficient oversight of labor. Host countries benefit not only from training received, a resource that can then be shared, but in observing how things are done and learning how to apply knowledge in new ways, otherwise known as *technology transfer*.

EconoTalk

When countries gain knowledge and skills from firms operating within their borders, it is called a **technology transfer.**

Multinational companies are not always enthusiastic about this. After having spent huge sums of time, money, and talent developing products and processes, having them copied or drawn on can be hard to swallow—especially if competing goods and services arise from the process.

Can't Get Past Comparisons

A good overall way to look at how multinationals pop up in different parts of the globe is as an extension of comparative advantage. What these firms hope to gain is a competitive advantage by seeking out and utilizing a less costly way of producing their products. For labor-intensive industries, that means finding a country with a large pool of inexpensive labor. For industries where knowledge and training are vital, the search is on for locations that feature potential employees with the right set of skills. The same applies to endeavors heavily reliant on natural resources or geography.

Labor on the Move

Between the increased speed and decreased cost of transportation, and the availability of cheap and instant communications, employees can both travel to where the jobs are and do them off-site and "mail it in."

Immigration laws put the brakes on mobility, of course, but as seen by the enormous illegal inflow of workers into the United States, people find ways to get to where the best opportunities are. This is only accelerated by the rising percentage of jobs, such as answering customer service calls, which can be done anywhere.

Because of this flexibility, it is not just workers in developing countries who have an issue with low pay. In the United States, Japan, Germany, and other wealthy countries, there are growing concerns that high-paying jobs will face competition from overseas. For example, a computer programmer in India makes about half what one in the United States does, so does that mean American wages for skilled workers are going to decline? It hasn't happened yet, but that doesn't end the worries that it might in the future.

The Least You Need to Know

◆ Multinationals are not just from the wealthy western countries any longer; more and more are venturing forth from countries such as China, India, and Russia.

◆ As multinationals continue to evolve, their organizational structures take on different forms. Instead of the old model where miniature versions of the home company are established abroad, it is becoming increasingly common to establish entire operations where the best combination of resources exists.

◆ Though sweatshops pay less than what workers in industrialized countries earn, both pay and working conditions are usually significantly higher than average for the country they reside in.

◆ With limits once imposed by distance and technology falling, labor is better able than ever to pursue the best available opportunities.

Part 4

Show Us the Money

Money used to be gold and silver, with paper representing these precious metals. Now, printing, multiplying, and borrowing money in many forms goes on in every country. Currency markets connect these currency dots and facilitate international trade and investment with puts, calls, strikes, and speculators. With all these hands in the international currency pie, currency values shift over time, gradually for countries with floating exchange rates, and sometimes abruptly where rates are fixed instead of market driven.

This part is devoted to how countries with different currencies are able to buy and sell goods and services from other countries around the world.

"Sorry, glass balls and colorful baubles just won't cut it anymore."

Does Money Really Make the World Go Around?

In This Chapter

- ◆ Money as a medium of exchange

- ◆ Attributing value to money

- ◆ The role of the Federal Reserve in American banking

What is worth very little on its own but can be traded for almost anything in the world, no matter how valuable? Money. Money can be whatever people agree it should be—anything from sea shells to painted rocks to beads. If money can be anything, then can't we just produce infinite amounts of it and buy our way to fantastic wealth? No; for though money can be anything, pumping out too much of it only does harm. In a global economy, countries wishing to participate must have sound money and manage it well. If they don't, then nobody will accept it. So how do modern economies manage money in a rapidly changing world? Read on and see.

Money Is as Money Does

Because money can be anything, anything used to perform its functions can be called money. As you read on, bear in mind the fundamental purpose of money: to allow individuals to trade what they have to offer for what they want. If you are a software engineer in India and want to buy coffee from Colombia, it would be hard to trade your skill for that product, especially given the distance involved. Maybe you could write a farmer a computer game that he would accept in return for a few hundred pounds of coffee beans, but arranging that would be pretty complicated. If the farmer can be paid in his country's currency after Indian currency has been exchanged for it, the process goes a lot more efficiently.

Making Exchanges Easier

Just imagine what you would have to go through if money weren't used in our economy. For whatever you wanted, you'd have to find something the owner of that item valued highly enough to trade you for it. Even going through that once could be pretty complicated, so just imagine if you were required to *barter* for everything you buy!

EconoTalk

Barter is a type of trade where goods and services are traded for other goods and services without using money.

Money's most important function is as a medium of exchange. If you are working in a fast-food restaurant, you don't want to get paid for your labor with bags of french fries; you want money in exchange for the work done, because you can then use it to buy things you want instead of, say, offering to grill 20 cheeseburgers for the owner of a store who sells shirts.

Not only do you want to be able to buy things with money in your own country, but things made in other countries have become increasingly important purchases. For this to happen, firms must have faith in a country's money. Not only does exchange between nations require that buyers and sellers come to a mutually beneficial agreement, it also requires that they agree about their respective currencies as reliable payment that can be exchanged for each other along with products.

Sound money is more important today than ever before. Because technology has lowered communication and transportation costs, we have access to an incredible array of goods and services offered by people in every corner of the globe. That means the money in your pocket needs to be trusted 5,000 miles away just as much as it is at the convenience store around the corner.

Keeping Score

Not only is money used as a medium of exchange, it is also good for tracking and recording the value of resources bought, sold, earned, and paid out, just as you might keep track of the distance traveled on the highway using miles. This allows us to value goods and services independently and to compare them to each other.

When we are paid in money and use it to purchase different items, we don't have to worry about how much work we have to do for a basket of groceries or how many bananas must be traded for a steak. Not only is money conducive to economic exchanges because of its ease of use, it is useful for measuring things such as national income, debts, and pay you have coming to you.

How Purchasing Power Travels Through Time

Money isn't just beneficial today; we can count on it in the future, as well. When you are paid, assuming you don't spend every cent immediately, you can save it, invest it, or hide it in your pillow to be spent at some point in the future.

One great thing about money is that it is the most liquid of all assets, which means it is the easiest to spend and get something else in exchange. You can go to the bank (or your favorite hiding spot) and take out your money and spend it easily. With cash machines and debit cards, it is possible now to spend your money around the clock—though sometimes the ease of use can lead to a whole new set of problems!

The Money Supply

We already know that anything, from whale's teeth to feathers, can be used as money, but did you know that there are different ways of counting the total amount of it available that yield vastly different results? How can that be? After all, counting the total number of paper bills, coins, painted rocks, or anything else should be a task that yields one total. It does seem that way at first, but when we look closer at how money is used, we see why counts of it can vary so much.

Easy Money

The easiest count of money to make is M1, and it is also the most narrowly defined: all *currency* in the hands of the public (anywhere in the world) plus all checking deposits in commercial banks and savings institutions. As of February 2007, total

EconoTalk

Currency is the total of coins and paper money. All coins in circulation are called **token money**.

American currency was $742.5 billion and total checkable deposits added up to $632.5 billion, which comes to a total M1 money supply of $1,375 billion.

The value of the metal in coins, or *token money*, is usually nowhere close to their face value. Part of the reason is that if the metals in coins came to be worth more than what could be purchased with them, coins would be melted down, sold, and thereby taken out of circulation. Most of our money comes in the form of paper Federal Reserve notes. These are issued by the Federal Reserve (the central bank of the United States) upon authorization by Congress.

It may sound strange at first to learn that checkable deposits are included in the money supply. Bear in mind, though, that all a check does is transfer ownership of money that is on deposit in financial institutions. It is also possible for individuals to turn checking deposits into cash at will. In many ways, checks are a better way of making payments than paper money. If paper money falls out of your pocket, you'll probably never see it again (and will have visions of somebody you've never seen before spending it happily). However, if a check is lost, there is less chance of losing money from it, because it requires your signature to work. Nobody puts cash in the mail, but most of us are fine with sending checks.

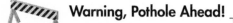

Warning, Pothole Ahead!

The money supply is never a static amount for any country. There are different ways to count the total supply that yield very different results, and the money supply—no matter how it is counted—is always shrinking or expanding.

A Growing Stash

The next definition of the money supply starts with M1 but is much broader. What expands the count here are categories that are very liquid, as currency is, but on their own do not meet the complete definition of a medium of exchange—these are known as *near-monies*.

The calculation for M2 is: M1 + savings deposits + time deposits below $100,000 + money market funds owned by individuals. Now let's take a closer look at the components of M2:

> **M1:** All currency in the hands of the public (anywhere in the world) plus all checking deposits in commercial banks and savings institutions.

Savings deposits: These include deposits in money market accounts and can be withdrawn in cash or transferred to checking accounts.

Small-time deposits (less than $100,000): These are things such as certificates of deposit, where a purchaser is rewarded with a higher rate of interest than is available on a regular savings account for leaving the money on deposit for a specific amount of time (such as a year). When time deposits mature, the money is available—and is available earlier if one is willing to pay a penalty charge to get hold of it.

Money market mutual funds owned by individuals: Similar to savings and time deposits, individuals can redeem these for cash or turn them into checkable deposits.

EconoTalk

Liquid financial assets that are not money but can easily be converted into currency or checkable deposits are called **near-monies**.

As of February 2007, the total money supply according to M2 was $6.7 trillion, about five times larger than M1!

Bump It Up Some More

In addition to M1 and M2, other definitions of money exist. One that is gaining in importance around the globe is MZM (money zero maturity). The focus here is on money that is immediately available at no cost. To calculate MZM, simply start with M2 and a) Subtract small-time deposits, because the maturity dates and penalties mean they are not available immediately without cost; and b) Add money market mutual funds owned by businesses, because checks can be written on these, and funds can be moved to and from them without penalty.

After the adjustments are made, MZM comes in a little bigger than M2, with a February 2007 total in the United States of $6.9 trillion. Though M1 is the easiest to understand, economists and bankers the world over generally use M2 and MZM.

Did You Know?

When you use a credit card, you are really borrowing money from whoever issued the credit card and will eventually repay it, along with interest to compensate the issuer for the loan. Debit cards, because they cause money to come directly out of your checking account balance, is more similar to money than credit cards, for your own money supply is immediately decreased.

What Gives Money Its Value?

You've probably heard people say "Have faith" before, but did you know that faith is the only thing that gives money its value and stability? Not faith in a Supreme Being, but faith in the government that backs a country's money. If a government does a poor job managing its money, faith drops and causes the value of the money to drop along with it. A government doing a good job managing its money experiences an increase in faith accompanied by a rise in its currency's value. The moral here is that if you want to make the most of your nation's money, be responsible with it.

Debts That Keep On Giving

If you were in charge of a country's money supply, the big reason for establishing good faith with everyone who uses the money is that your currency and checkable deposits are nothing more than promises to pay. And a promise is only as good as the word of whoever makes it. In the United States, our money is simply debts of the Federal Reserve that are in circulation, and checks written represent debts of banking institutions.

Did You Know? _____

The Federal Reserve System (the "Fed") is the central bank of the United States and is made up of a Board of Governors and 12 Federal Reserve Banks spread around the country. It's the Fed's job to oversee the American banking system and manage the money with the goal of promoting full employment and steady, healthy economic growth while promoting stable prices. Now there's an ambitious job!

In the past, it was common for economies to back up their money with something of market value, most commonly gold. Those days are long gone. There is nowhere you can go and turn in your dollars for a specific amount of gold—though you can use your money to buy gold. Today governments have to manage their money according to the level of economic activity they engage in, both at home and abroad.

Why Money Matters

If our currency and coins have no intrinsic value, what makes them more valuable than play money? A combination of three following things do the job: money's status as legal tender, its acceptability, and its scarcity.

Legal Tender: All paper money in the United States has a statement saying "This note is legal tender for all debts, public and private." With the government decreeing its money to be the only legal tender with no other forms competing, its status is assured (so long as the government is functioning).

Acceptability: Going along with what was just said, knowing that money will be accepted in exchange for goods and services is vital. For example, would you take a job if you had doubts about whether you could buy anything with the money you were to be paid?

Scarcity: Just as we learned earlier, the interactions of supply and demand determine how much an item is worth. Because governments reserve the right to issue money, they have control over the supply. If there is a fairly predictable demand for a particular currency, the supply provided by the government will determine its purchasing power.

> **Warning, Pothole Ahead!**
>
> Just because money has no value independent of its function and can be issued only by a country's government does not mean the government can get away with printing huge amounts of it. All this does is cause the value to drop and possibly damage it further through an erosion of trust.

The Powers of Purchase

You can imagine the temptation to "sneak" more money into circulation in the attempt to increase wealth. When the government expands the money supply, the value of money drops. But those who receive the money first can spend it to purchase goods and services before it loses value.

Money's *purchasing power* depends on the price level in the economies where it is used (or exchanged). The higher the price level, the less each monetary unit is worth. The lower the price level, the more each monetary unit is worth. No matter what country they live in, what consumers like to see is a

> **EconoTalk**
>
> The amount of goods and services money can buy is its **purchasing power**.

stable price level while their incomes go up, which means they can buy more of the goods and services they desire. What nobody likes is having the price level rise faster than income, which means less and less can be acquired in exchange for one's money.

Eating Away at Money

A term for describing what happens when the price level rises and the value of money drops is *inflation*. When inflation occurs, it takes more money than it did before to buy the same amount of goods and services. Inflation isn't a big deal if incomes rise faster. In most of the world's economies, it is assumed that there will be some inflation. Indeed, inflation of 2 or 3 percent is usually considered well within an acceptable rate. The problems occur when inflation gets out of hand, say at 15 percent a year or more, and incomes can't keep pace and faith in the currency is lost. But even modest inflation adds up, and average goods that cost $100 in 1996 cost $128 by 2006. Or, if you earned $30,000 in 1996 and earn $38,393 today, you haven't really had a pay increase in terms of purchasing power. Inflation was much worse between 1976 and 1986. (What cost $100 in 1976 on average cost $200 by 1986!)

Did You Know?

Hyperinflation is the term used to describe an especially dramatic rate of inflation. As you can imagine, the rapid drop in purchasing power can have a very destabilizing effect in any country experiencing it. For example, in 1923, when inflation in Germany was at its worst, it took a wheelbarrow full of marks to buy a newspaper! By this time, workers had gotten in the habit of spending their money immediately after getting paid, for by the next day it could well be worth even less than it was at present. In Germany, the price level had doubled between 1914 and 1919. In just the first five months of 1922, it doubled again. Beer went from 5.6 marks a liter to 18; milk went from 7 marks a liter to 16. These kinds of price jumps were experienced throughout the economy. Wages, however, came nowhere close to keeping up. For the Nazis, this disastrous hyperinflation was a golden opportunity.

Functions of the Federal Reserve

In the United States, it came to pass early in the twentieth century that a central bank, the Federal Reserve, was created to manage the banking system. Because almost all other countries have something similar, the following outline the different functions of the Federal Reserve.

The Banker's Bank: A primary purpose of the Federal Reserve and most other central banks is to function as a "banker's bank." This translates into the central banks doing for local banks what local banks do for their customers. The

Federal Reserve, then, accepts deposits from and makes loans to its member banks. Under extreme conditions the Fed is a "banker of last resort" and will help out local banks that are in serious financial trouble.

When the Big Dog Barks: The Federal Reserve is responsible for managing the country's money supply and keeping the dollar stable. One way of doing this is to try to influence the supply and demand of currency. So if the Fed decides it's time to stimulate the economy with fresh injections of dollars, what does it do? It buys government securities from member banks to put more money into the economy. And if it's time to slow down the rate of growth or keep inflation from getting out of hand? The Fed sells government securities to "soak up" currency, thereby reducing the supply and increasing its purchasing power.

Managing Interest Rates: Another tool of the Federal Reserve tries to influence interest rates in the economy. They don't do this directly but rather through signaling their intentions through the rates they charge member banks to borrow from them. This rate, with some additional interest tacked on for profit's sake, is then charged to bank clients. Most lending, of course, is done through private financial institutions. All the largest are multinational organizations that deal with central banks from a multitude of countries.

The Least You Need to Know

- We don't pursue money just to accumulate piles of it; money makes it possible to efficiently exchange what we produce for what we want. In this way, money serves as a medium of exchange.

- Money also serves as a store of value. But in order to service this purpose, others in society have to have faith in the value of money.

- Each country's money supply is defined in different ways, and varies greatly according to how it is counted and the economic conditions.

- The Federal Reserve was created to manage banking in America. The Fed does everything from trying to influence interest rates to stimulating the economy with more dollars.

Chapter 12

The Power to Create— Money, That Is

In This Chapter

- ◆ Checkable deposits and the fractional reserve banking system
- ◆ How countries use money to exchange goods and services
- ◆ America's national deficit

In the previous chapter, we looked at the different values of money and its use as a medium of exchange. This chapter takes the discussions a step further and answers questions such as: How do we make money? How do we track the money that goes in and comes out of a country? We also take a look at the United States' monetary deficit. Is there a way to reverse the deficit, and are competing countries with account surpluses a serious threat to the U.S. economy?

How Money Is Created

Sure, paper money and coins are printed and minted by governments, but we have already seen that the money supply is much larger than the physical count of these. So who ups the ante—who makes the multiplying happen? Banks and thrifts do in the form of checkable deposits.

Fraction Action

In most countries, their central banks operate a fractional reserve banking system, which requires that only a fraction of the money on deposit with them stays in the vaults or on deposit with the central bank. The rest can be loaned out. This means, as you will see in the next section, that a dollar does its duty many times over—and that is why the money supply is so much greater than the physical quantity of money.

The Gold Diggers

Early global traders had a problem: they traveled with gold or other precious metals to pay for goods or as earnings from goods they sold. This made them prime targets for those who would rather rob than toil. Not only that, but every time gold changed hands it would have to be weighed and its purity confirmed. A more efficient alternative was developed during the sixteenth century; goldsmiths would keep it on deposit for a fee and give the depositors receipts so they could reclaim it in the future. So early forms of paper money made the scene.

At first, paper receipts stood for exactly the amount of gold on deposit. Before long, though, goldsmiths realized that there was much more gold on deposit than was claimed at any one time, especially because it had become more common for people to trade gold receipts than gold itself. From there, the practice arose of issuing receipts in excess of gold holdings. These were doled out as loans, and interest was charged for them. Merchants were willing to take out these loans and pay the interest because the receipts were, after all, backed with gold. If everybody with gold on deposit showed up at the same time to reclaim it, there would have been a problem, but the odds were usually against it—though panics did occur occasionally and caught goldsmiths and early banks short.

Creating More Money by Loaning It Out

If you have a bank and your clients deposit $100 with you, the money supply can be doubled simply by loaning it to somebody else. Maybe the person who borrowed it spends part of it and leaves the rest in his own bank account, which is then loaned to somebody else, and so the process goes. A complete discussion of money and the banking system is beyond this book's mandate, but if you read through the following table, you will get a general idea of how an initial sum of currency can be "grown" into a much bigger money supply.

In this table, Bank #1 receives a deposit of $200. It must keep 20 percent on hand as reserves, but can loan out the rest, which then goes into another bank's account, then another's and … you get the idea. The final figure at the bottom-right corner is the total amount of new money created.

Bank	Deposit	Reserve	Loaned
#1	200	40	160
#2	160	32	128
#3	128	26	102
#4	102	20	80
#5	80	16	64
#6	64	13	51
#7	51	10	41
#8	41	8	33
#9	33	6	27
#10	27	5	<u>22</u>
Total money created			$708

Why Money Multiplies Faster Than Rabbits

In the previous table, we see that banking systems take money in excess of their reserve requirements and create new money by loaning it out. The same effect is seen when the world's households spend the money they earned as income, which then becomes the income of other households. These households then spend it and, in turn, another household has income.

In both cases, the process only works when there is significant faith in the value of the money involved and the abilities of the respective governments involved to back it up. A natural question here is this: What happens when faith falters and money is not spent or loaned? If existing loans are paid off faster than new ones are made, the money supply shrinks, just as it does if households no longer accept money from other households.

Tracking International Monetary Transactions

Now that you've been introduced to what money is and does and how it is created, destroyed, expanded, and contracted, it's time to look at how countries use it to exchange goods and services with each other. Every nation wants to know just how much money comes in and goes out, along with what it is spent on and the activities that earn it.

Accounting for Money's Movements

The great thing about double-entry bookkeeping is that it is one of the few places where the rules dictate that balance is always maintained. Problems arise in the interpretation, especially when one side of the equation is looked at closely while the other is ignored. We'll be fair and balanced and show you how to look at both sides.

> **Warning, Pothole Ahead!**
>
> In a double-entry accounting system, be it for a solitary small business, a huge corporation, a nation, or the entire world, the total value of the debits recorded *always* equals the total value of the credits. The same applies to every individual exchange of resources as well.

Inflows from other countries in the form of payments that are recorded as credits include:

The sale of goods (exports)

Income on investments held abroad

Travel payments

Foreign aid

Investments from foreign nations

Gifts from foreign nations

Outflows to other countries in the form of payments recorded as debits include:

The purchase of goods (imports)

Aid given to foreign nations

Investments made in foreign countries

Gifts to residents of foreign nations

With all the talk of debits and credits, it is important to remember that in every case, exchanges are involved where each party incurs both credits and debits. Remember, nothing comes without sacrifice, and this is what accounting systems were designed to chronicle.

The Current Account

The current account tracks the monetary value of exchanges between countries in goods, services, investment income, and unilateral transfers of money. Let's look at each one in more detail.

Exchanges in goods include all the exports and imports of things such as automobiles, clothing, fuel, food, software, and so on. When these are recorded, the money received for exports is recorded as positive numbers, which are credits; and the money going out as negative numbers, which are debits. When exports exceed imports, there is a merchandise trade surplus; when exports are less than imports, there is a merchandise trade deficit.

Exchanges in services include things such as banking, insurance, consulting, legal, and technical goods. In other words, services can be anything not tangible in the sense that goods are. As with goods, there is a surplus when exports exceed imports and a deficit when exports are less than imports. The same holds true for income received from foreign countries and income paid to them, as it does for transfers of tangible or financial assets from one country to another.

From all the preceding items, the current account is calculated. It is the most widely quoted balance of all those included in a nation's balance of payments. Problems arise when it is looked at in isolation, as with the final score of a basketball game where whoever gets the most points (surplus) beats the opponent who has fewer points (deficit). Instead of looking at it as a standalone number, the current account should be examined in conjunction with the capital account, which gives us what Paul Harvey calls "the rest of the story," or the other side of the accounting equation.

Remember, too, that it makes a difference what kinds of goods get exchanged between countries. When Japanese companies ship tens of millions of DVD players made in China to the United States, their value is added to the merchandise trade deficit. But when McDonald's and Starbucks sell tens of millions of hamburgers and lattés in China, these generally don't get shipped from the United States (they would get cold, for one thing). Instead, supplies are purchased in China or other countries and the profits from McDonald's, Starbucks, and other U.S. multinational operations tend to flow back to the United States.

What Goes Out Must Come Back: The Capital Account

The capital and financial account is, in comparison to the current account, a neglected member of the balance of payments family. It is no less important for the lack of attention, however, for it records all international sales and purchases of assets. The vast majority of these concern financial transactions such as investments in stocks, bonds, property, and businesses—that is what we will focus on here.

Keep in mind that money is a debt obligation, so that when a dollar, or any other country's currency, goes abroad to purchase a foreign-made good or service, it doesn't just sit there. Much as with a coupon, currency needs to be redeemed to fulfill its mission. This means it must be traded for something. A country awash in American dollars from export sales is likely to invest those same dollars in American assets. And why not? The U.S. economy is a global powerhouse, and its financial markets are the safest places to invest money and earn a reasonable return on it.

What all this means is that the deficit in the current account that arose from Americans buying more from other countries than they buy from us comes back, in large part, in the form of surplus investment in American assets. This surplus is the result of foreign nations investing more in America than America does in them.

Following is the United States' balance of payments for 2004. Note how closely the surplus in incoming investments (net financial transactions) mirrors the deficit in the merchandise trade balance. Note also that the accounts are in balance. (Amounts shown in parentheses are negative.)

Balance of Payments in the United States in 2004

Current Account	Dollar Amount in Billions
Imports	(1,263.2)
Exports	<u>713.8</u>
Merchandise trade balance	(549.4)
Travel and transportation, net	(9.3)
Military transactions, net	(10.9)
Royalties and licensing, net	28.0
Other services, net	<u>51.4</u>
Services balance	<u>59.2</u>

Current Account	Dollar Amount in Billions
Goods and services balance	(490.2)
Investment income, net	21.9
Employee compensation, net	(5.3)
Income balance	16.6
Government grants	(21.8)
Government pensions	(5.3)
Private remittances	(41.1)
Unilateral transfers balance	(68.2)
Current account balance	(541.8)
Capital and Financial Account	
Capital account transactions, net	(3.1)
Financial account transactions, net	579.0
Statistical discrepancy	(34.1)
Capital and financial account balance	541.8

Source: United States Department of Commerce

What Do the Accounts Mean for Us?

Given that the balance of payments does balance out, why is so much attention paid to one part of it? For one thing, it is easier to grasp the trade in goods than it is investments. All of us see foreign-made goods on the shelves when we go shopping and are well aware that we spend more and more money on these. What most of us do not come into contact with daily are inflows and outflows of money being invested. In other words, it's easier to relate to the sale of a microwave oven than a government bond.

Warning, Pothole Ahead! _____

A current account deficit must be offset by a surplus in the capital and financial account. To look at one without the other is to come away with an unbalance—an inaccurate point of view.

Buying More Than We Sell

One thing that rankles many Americans is the United States' status as the country with the world's largest current account deficit. Being the world's largest economy means that this needn't be too great a shock, but it is if you assume a positive balance is better than a negative one. A current account deficit can be painful in some sectors of the economy. If, for example, you were employed in a television factory that was shut down because Americans chose to buy cheaper televisions from South Korea, you, your co-workers, and the factory owners suffer. At the same time, consumers benefit from being able to purchase cheaper televisions and have money left over to spend on other things.

As much attention as is paid to job losses resulting from imports, little notice is given to how this promotes the creation of new businesses, jobs, and wealth. Say some of the American money that went abroad comes back in the form of an investment made in stocks issued by a new American company. That company uses the money to set up shop and pay American workers who, in turn, buy more American goods and services—in addition to spending on foreign products and possibly contributing to additional future investments in the United States. So things do balance out; it's just easier to see the losses than the gains.

The last year the United States experienced a surplus in its current account balance was 1980, a *mere* $2.4 billion. The following are current account balances for the United States for select years since 1980. Bear in mind that these deficits are mirrored by capital account surpluses, but these are examined with much less frequency. (Amounts shown in parentheses are negative.)

Year	Current Account Balance (in Billions of Dollars)
1982	(11.5)
1986	(151.2)
1992	(67.9)
1996	(129.2)
2002	(480.9)
2006	(829.1)

Source: U.S. Department of Commerce, Bureau of Economic Analysis

Now, at the same time the United States is cranking out bigger current account deficits, there are other countries with growing current account surpluses. What really scares some people is when they see an emerging economy, such as China, running up staggering surpluses. The natural fear is that this represents a loss of economy activity to China, and that the United States will soon be overtaken. Again, the increasing investment coming back to America is rarely considered.

In this table, you can see a select list of current account balances for trading members of the global economy. (Amounts shown in parentheses are negative.)

Country	Current Account Balance (in Billions of Dollars)
People's Republic of China (PRC)	179.1
Japan	174.4
Germany	134.8
Russia	105.3
Switzerland	50.4
United Arab Emirates	26.8
Hong Kong	20.9
Canada	20.5
Iraq	8.1
India	(26.4)
France	(38.0)
United Kingdom	(57.6)
Spain	(98.6)
United States	(862.3)

The World Factbook, *2006*

You Can Go Back: The Capital Account

Are there any mechanisms, aside from direct government intervention, that can reverse the deficit? Because the deficit is pretty much offset by surplus investment, if foreigners see American markets as losing their luster for any reason, and if better investment opportunities are available in a world where capital is ever more mobile, then the inflow will drop. Without this money coming in, there will be less going out (the balance of payments must remain balanced). Americans would purchase fewer exports and the value of the dollar would drop on the world market. This drop would translate to lower prices for American goods and probably result in the growth of export sales. The outcome, then, could be a current account surplus and a capital account deficit. After all, it has happened before.

A deep recession could quickly cure the merchandise trade deficit. When millions are thrown out of work, they buy less imported merchandise. And when the economy tanks, investors overseas cut back their investments. Of course this "medicine" is far worse than the alleged deficit disease.

So How Bad a Problem Is the Deficit?

The current account deficit is neither good nor bad by itself. For Americans worried about competing with other nations, issues such as productivity, innovation, and entrepreneurship are far more important. Healthy long-term economic growth supported by a well-managed money supply and economic policies are what will guarantee increased wealth far into the future. The deficit, in comparison, barely matters.

The Least You Need to Know

- ◆ The money supply increases when banks loan out money they have on deposit.

- ◆ Countries use national accounting systems that maintain balance through the use of debits and credits.

- ◆ A current account deficit will be offset by a surplus of investment shown in the capital account.

- ◆ Promoting the overall health of an economy through wise policies and management is much more important than total imports or exports.

Chapter 13

Money Matters Everywhere: Foreign Exchange

In This Chapter

◆ Learning the foreign exchange market

◆ Determining market forces and exchange rates

◆ Having supply, demand, and equilibrium

◆ Speculating on exchange

A fascinating aspect of the global economy is the variety of currencies used by different nations. Be it a dollar, peso, euro, konar, franc, or yen, people want to buy goods and services with them. Not just goods and services produced at home, either, but a variety from around the world. Because one country's currency is going to be used to buy products from other countries with different currencies, it's necessary to have mechanisms in place for exchanging currencies.

The Foreign Exchange Market

To facilitate citizens, businesses, and governments from different countries trading with each other, foreign exchange markets developed. These markets exist wherever foreign currencies and debt instruments are bought and sold. Only a small portion of exchanges involve actual currency itself—mostly just the paper and coins you carry around in your pockets and purses. Most of what goes on is the transfer of bank deposits. The world's major banks keep inventories of foreign exchange on hand in their branches and correspondent banks in many different countries and make it available for purchase.

Large and Liquid

There is no economic market that compares with foreign exchange in size. Worldwide, daily foreign exchange transactions top an average of $1.5 trillion. Single trades can be in the hundreds of millions of dollars. Because these markets are interconnected electronically, and so much money is involved, prices of different currencies are changing constantly, sometimes as often as 25 times in a single minute.

Not all currencies are for sale in foreign exchange markets (though most are). If a country, usually small, does not produce things other parties want, then there is no point in keeping their currency on hand. In addition, factors such as political upheaval and bad economic times cause other members of the global community to shy away from a particular currency. You can see why, then, any country seeking acceptance as a trading member of the global economy has a strong incentive to "get its house in order."

The foreign exchange market is dispersed. There is no mandated structure, organization, or central authority that operates it as there is for stock exchanges. Nor are there limits on where the market operates or the currencies available (or not available). The foreign exchange market, then, exists wherever currencies are being traded, with the world's biggest exchanges located in New York, London, and Tokyo, and also large ones in places such as Frankfurt and Chicago. Given the differences in time zones, it's possible to find an exchange open for business almost anytime, day or night. So if you get a yen for a franc during the night, you can probably find a place to satisfy it!

When Argentina's government closed down banks in 2002 and halted formal convertibility from the Argentine peso to the dollar, currency markets moved out into the streets. Walking along certain downtown streets, you would hear quiet voices calling "Cambio, cambio" ("Swap, swap" in Spanish). Closing formal currency exchanges encouraged informal markets as currency exchange "arbolitos" (meaning "little trees" in Spanish, since they "sprouted" green dollars), which offered to exchange pesos for dollars. And though the government can try to fix exchange rates by decree, markets discover them through ongoing supply and demand for currencies.

Following is a list of the top 10 banks operating in the worldwide foreign exchange market:

Bank	% Share of Foreign Exchange Market
Deutsche Bank	19.30
UBS AG	14.85
Citi	9.00
Royal Bank of Scotland	8.90
Barclays Capital	8.80
Bank of America	5.29
HSBC	4.36
Goldman Sachs	4.14
JPMorgan	3.33
Morgan Stanley	2.86

Source: Euromoney FX Poll, 2007

Currency on the Spot

The simplest way to acquire foreign currency is through a direct purchase, called a *spot transaction*. Delivery is immediate (by the second business day after the transaction) and you go off with another country's money.

Planning Ahead

Sometimes a deal is made for foreign currency well in advance of the actual date it is needed. And why do that? Say you plan on making a big purchase from China in a few months but are worried that acquiring Chinese currency is going to be more expensive when you need it. Instead of just waiting and worrying, you can contract with a bank to buy those yuan in the future at a specific price. You have to pay for the right, of course, and maybe provide some collateral. But if your worries prove accurate, it's worth it—if you weren't correct, the cost probably wasn't too steep anyway.

Planning ahead with a *forward transaction* gives you a span of time that goes from anything longer than the two-business-day spot purchase to months or years into the future.

EconoTalk _____

The purchase of foreign exchange for cash when the transaction is completed within two days is a **spot transaction**.

A **forward transaction** occurs when a specific amount of currency is contracted for but not paid for or received until a later date.

A Temporary Trade

Given the enormous sums of money banks engaged in the foreign exchange market work with, it is no surprise that they can run short of particular currencies or have surpluses of them. What is the solution? Those with too little and those with too much can get together and make *currency swaps*.

EconoTalk _____

A **currency swap** takes place when banks convert one currency to another with the understanding that they will convert back at a particular time in the future.

For example, Bank A is awash in more pesos than it can use but needs dollars badly. Bank B has plenty of dollars but worries that there aren't enough pesos on hand to meet customer demand. With members of the foreign exchange markets linked together electronically, it's not hard for Bank A and Bank B to find each other, and a swap is born.

From Bank to Bank

The majority of banks don't count trading in foreign currency as a big part of the business they do. They have connections with correspondent banks they can take advantage of when the need arises. Usually they just need assistance with retail transactions, which are sales to consumers of less than one million units of a particular currency.

Wholesale transactions are those that exceed one million units of a currency and usually are deals made between banks.

Easier Than Reading Tea Leaves

If you're ever curious, you can probably find foreign exchange rates printed in your daily newspaper. (And of course you can quickly find them on the Internet.) Remember, these change often, so if you're thinking of buying foreign exchange, check first—the rate might be a lot different than it was the last time you looked.

The foreign exchange quotations could tell you, for example, that it takes 3 units of Country X's money to purchase 1 unit of Country Y's, or that .5 units of Country Y's money gets you 1 unit of Country Z's.

Did You Know? _____

The exchange rate tells you how much of a particular currency must be sacrificed to get one unit of another currency.

If you want a little more detail while thumbing through the pages, you can look at how different major currencies did on the forward market the previous day. What this schedule does is show you how much of different foreign currencies can be purchased for American dollars. It provides different dates for future delivery, too: the third Wednesday of the next March, June, September, and December. Further, you can see at what rate particular currencies have opened (price at the day's start), how high the price went, how low it got, at what rate it closed for the day, and its lifetime highs and lows. Not only do you see what a currency is going for, but also how volatile it was on the day you are scanning.

Opting for an Option

What if you're concerned about the price of a currency you'll need in the future but don't want to commit to a forward transaction? No problem; just purchase the ability to buy currency at a set price to protect yourself in case it gets too expensive. An option is purchased so that the buyer has the right to buy or sell financial instruments during a set time period in the future. There is no requirement that the option be exercised.

You might not need the option, of course, but it could come in handy and save, or earn, you a significant amount of money—and it might help you sleep better at night, too. The two different types of options are as follows:

A *call option* enables you to buy foreign currency at a set price.

A *put option* enables you to sell foreign currency at a set price.

Speculators purchase calls and puts in hopes of buying and selling currencies at a profit and succeed according to how accurate their predictions of future currency movements are.

Market Forces and Exchange Rates

The worldwide exchange market is an excellent example of how equilibrium prices are set by the forces of supply and demand in a free market. It is easy to understand why countries sometimes succumb to temptation and intervene to lend their currency a helping (meddling) hand; the free market does not always express the opinion you want it to.

The Demand for Other People's Money

What happens when the United States buys goods from China? Lots of things, but one of them is that a demand for Chinese currency rises. As we learned before, the lower the price of Chinese currency (meaning the less American dollars have to be sacrificed for it), the more that will be purchased to buy those low-priced goods. If Chinese currency becomes more expensive (more American dollars have to be sacrificed to acquire it), less of it and the Chinese goods it buys will be purchased.

> **Warning, Pothole Ahead!**
>
> It's not just the market price of a foreign currency that determines how much of it is purchased. The value of the currency being used for the purchase is also important; the higher its value, the more it can be traded for; the lower its value, the less it can be traded for.

Finding Equilibrium—For Now

Just as with any other economic market, the interests of buyers and sellers in the foreign exchange market are at odds: buyers want the cheapest prices and sellers want to charge the most they possibly can. Neither side of the exchange will get what they want, but they will agree on a compromise price, the equilibrium point, which allows both to benefit from the transaction—even if they don't benefit as much as they'd like.

As you know, equilibrium is not forever, and anything that changes either supply or demand will lead to a new equilibrium point. For example, if the demand for the currency goes up, the demand curve will shift up and to the right, which means it now costs more and the currency being used to buy is worth less in comparison. A move down and to the left means the opposite: the currency is cheaper and the other country's currency is more expensive in comparison (see Chapter 3 for more on supply and demand curves).

Can a Weak Currency Ever Win?

It's natural for citizens of a country to want a "strong" currency—one that doesn't come cheap and is valued highly around the world, but being weak has its advantages. For example, if you sell goods to a country whose currency has become more expensive relative to yours, your goods are now cheaper in comparison to the local competition, so sales may go up. If your currency suddenly rises in value, though, your goods become more expensive in comparison to the competition and sales could suffer.

Good things that happen when a currency *appreciates:*

 EconoTalk

A currency **appreciates** when its costs in terms of other currencies goes up. A currency **depreciates** when its costs in terms of other currencies drops.

- ◆ Foreign goods become cheaper, which also helps keep inflation lower.

- ◆ It costs less to travel in other countries.

Bad things that happen when a currency appreciates:

- ◆ Cheaper imported foreign goods may mean lower sales of competing goods produced domestically.

- ◆ Exports to other countries are more expensive, which may also mean a loss of sales.

- ◆ Tourism in and travel to the United States may decline as it becomes more expensive for people coming from abroad.

Good things that happen happen when a currency *depreciates:*

- ◆ Sales of exported goods go up when they become cheaper in comparison to the local competition.

- ◆ Tourism in and travel to the United States increases as it becomes cheaper for people from other nations.

Bad things that happen when a currency depreciates:

- ◆ Foreign-made goods become more expensive.

- ◆ Travel costs to other countries go up.

- ◆ More expensive foreign goods put upward pressure on inflation.

Whenever a currency appreciates or depreciates significantly, it disrupts the long-term plans of businesses involved in international trade. Neither businessmen nor travelers like surprises, particularly those that raise expenses or reduce revenue. That is why firms with extensive international business enter currency markets to ensure against adverse currency shifts.

The Least You Need to Know

- ◆ Foreign goods must be purchased with foreign currency.

- ◆ Not only does a currency's value fluctuate in its home country, but what it's worth in terms of other country's currencies also fluctuates.

- ◆ A currency becoming stronger or becoming weaker is not all good or all bad.

- ◆ Supply and demand determines money's value in the worldwide foreign exchange market.

Chapter 14

Determining Exchange Rates

In This Chapter

- How supply and demand establish exchange rates
- Looking at exchange rates in the long run
- Buying and selling in the short run
- The benefit of currency speculators to world trade

Have you ever heard a coach talking about how important it is that his players keep up on the fundamentals of the game, that these simple things determine the outcome of the contest, no matter how grand the strategy? The same is true for money.

You Mean It's More Than Supply and Demand?

International exchange used to be based on a gold standard. Major currencies were backed by gold, and large stockpiles of gold stored in Fort Knox and other secure locations could be shipped from country to country to balance trade and currencies. Economists still debate the strengths and weaknesses of a gold standard (skeptics ask, "Why dig up gold in one place so you can bury it somewhere else?"). But when currency was defined as a fixed weight of gold, it was difficult for central banks to print more paper currency than could be backed up with gold reserves.

Currencies backed by gold held their value over many decades. A managed exchange system was established at the Bretton Woods Conference near the end of World War II, and gold played a minor role in the new monetary order until the 1970s.

How well has the dollar held its value as a "fiat" or paper currency no longer backed by gold? Motel 6 offers one clue. The chain has upgraded its rooms over the years, but few realize its name used to be its nightly room rate. The Consumer Price Index (CPI) measures the rate of inflation (the rate at which the dollar's value has diminished over time). A $40-a-night room at Motel 6 in 2007, adjusted for inflation, would have been about $6 in 1962, the year Motel 6 was founded.

The powerful economies of the developed world adopted "floating" exchange rates in the early 1970s, where supply and demand for currencies established exchange rates. Despite fears that completely abandoning the gold standard would lead to economic instability and even crisis, the system has worked out pretty well overall; though the United States experienced fairly high inflation through the 1970s, followed by a severe recession in the early 1980s, inflation rates have been modest since then. There can be significant swings in a currency's value in a short period of time, even a few hours, but in the long run the changes have been gentler and generally within normal ranges.

Beyond the Curves

In Chapter 16, you learned how supply and demand set equilibrium prices for different currencies, but it's important to add a deeper understanding of the *market fundamentals* that influence the forces of supply and demand.

 EconoTalk

Consumer choice, government policy, productivity, inflation, and interest rates are important **market fundamentals** that influence supply and demand.

Through a Crystal Ball Darkly

With so much money changing hands and so many buyers and sellers from all over the globe participating and trying to get the best deals possible, the foreign currency market is very efficient at gathering and processing information that provides insight into how well or poorly a currency is doing, or may do in the future. As with purchases of stock, it's not so much what is going on at present but what investors predict for the days ahead that matters, so any tea leaves around for the reading will be scanned carefully.

Warning, Pothole Ahead!

Expectations are what traders in the currency market think will happen in the future and usually have more to do with the predicted price of money than whatever is going on at present.

Exchange Rates in the Long Run

With currency values floating, supply and demand forces can shift their values significantly over the long run. The dollar was worth 20 percent more than the Euro in 2002, and by October 2007 it was worth 30 percent less. That is a 50 percent shift in value over just five years in the world's two major currencies. Needless to say, both businesses and tourists notice when prices jump or fall this sharply. Short-term factors can push currencies in a direction opposite of where the long-run influences point. How can this be? Temporary fluctuations in things such as interest rates, for example, are significant in a transaction made in the present, but these ups and downs do not set the future, nor do medium-run factors.

What really matters in the long run are consumer tastes, trade policy, productivity, and price levels. Their impact is summarized in the following and then examined in more detail in the next section.

What Goes Up Must Come Down?

When consumer tastes shift to purchase more imports, demand for foreign currencies rise, which puts downward pressure on the value of the local currency.

When consumer tastes of imports drops, demand for foreign currency falls, which puts upward pressure on the local currency value.

When trade restrictions are reduced, consumers purchase more imports, raising demand for foreign currency putting downward pressure on local currency values.

When trade restrictions are increased, consumers purchase fewer imports, reducing demand for foreign currencies and pushing local currency values up.

When productivity declines, local goods are less competitive with imports and less are sold overseas, lowering demand for the local currency and pushing its value down.

When productivity increases, local goods are more competitive with imports and more are sold overseas, pushing the value of the currency up.

Imports, Exports, and Buying Power

Say Americans become convinced that something about the yeast in beers brewed in Australia leads to longer life and begin buying mass quantities of it. The resulting increase in demand for Australian currency makes it go up in value, with American dollars depreciating against it because fewer Australian dollars can be purchased per American dollar.

What would happen if it were discovered in the future that beer in general causes toenails to grow excessively? The demand for Australian currency would drop, and American dollars would appreciate against it. In the same way, increased demand for American dollars makes them appreciate, and a drop in demand makes them depreciate. These rules' long-run effects on exchange rates can be summarized as follows: increased demand for a country's exports cause its currency to rise in value; falling demand for a country's exports causes its currency to drop in value.

Rates Go Up with the Barricades

Trade policies have a significant impact on exchange rates because they exert influence over the demand for currencies from other nations. For example, let's look at what would happen if the United States imposed steep tariffs on beef imported from Brazil. Because the tariff makes Brazilian beef prices go up, American consumers buy less of the meat and therefore need fewer Brazilian dollars. When the demand for Brazil's currency drops, the American dollar appreciates (meaning you can buy more Brazilian currency).

On the other hand, say a new administration comes into power after the next election and gets rid of tariffs on Brazilian beef. With its price now lower, American consumers buy more of it. Because this calls for buying more Brazilian currency to pay for all those steaks, demand goes up and the currency rises in price. This means the American dollar depreciates (meaning you can buy less Brazilian currency with it).

Productivity and Purchasing Power

Not only can *productivity* be measured by individual products, it is also calculated for nations as a whole. A rise in productivity means that more can be produced with the same resources. Producers can increase sales domestically and abroad by lowering prices, and increased sales abroad increases demand for the currency. If more of a country's products are being purchased worldwide, the demand for their currency rises, and its value appreciates.

The same thing also works the other way. Say that Country A's productivity remains stagnant while Countries B, C, and so on all experience productivity gains. Demand then drops for Country A's goods and services and fewer of its monetary units need to be purchased. As you know by now, this decrease in demand leads to a depreciation of Country A's currency.

EconoTalk

Productivity is the amount of a good or service that can be produced per hour of labor.

What Goes Up Rarely Comes Back Down

What would happen if prices in Canada went up significantly while prices in the American economy remained stable? Canadians would find many American products to be a better bargain now than they used to be, so sales of them would rise in Canada. This in turn means Canada needs to buy more American dollars, whose price is pushed up by the increased demand.

If Canadian prices then dropped in comparison to American prices, the opposite would occur. Now Canadian products are a better deal and Americans buy more of them. The demand for Canadian dollars rises and pushes the price of Canadian currency to do the same.

Parity in Purchasing

According to the law of one price, in free markets (no barriers to trade) with no transportation costs and with information easily available, the price of the same item in different countries should—when currencies are converted—be the same, at least in theory.

Transportation costs can be significant, though, as can trade barriers. If sneakers, for example, were significantly cheaper in Bolivia than Iceland, some ambitious person would spot the opportunity and buy hordes of sneakers in Bolivia at the low prices and sell them at a profit in Iceland. This would drive up prices in Bolivia and dampen them in Iceland until sneakers could be found for the same price in both countries.

Merchants facing competition from another country where prices are low can turn to political means to try to protect their profits. If the merchant's government can be convinced low-priced imports are unfair and bad for business, letting local money and jobs slip away to foreign competitors, that's when the tariffs and quotas come in.

Did You Know? _____

The theory of purchasing power parity asserts that the prices of goods and services sold in different locations around the globe will make adjustments until they are equal everywhere.

A simple test of the law of one price is provided every month by *The Economist* magazine. It is not an ideal test of the theory, because the price of the good used contains costs such as labor and rent that cannot simply be bought in one place and sent to another. At the same time, however, this limitation introduces a useful element of reality in looking at how the theory works out in practice. The good used by *The Economist* is a Big Mac. The following chart takes selected countries from the index and shows the Big Mac price in local currency, in American dollars, the actual exchange rate, and how much the local currency is undervalued or overvalued against the dollar:

Big Mac Index

Country	Big Mac Price in Dollars	% Local Currency Is Undervalued or Overvalued
United States	3.22	
Australia	2.67	-17
Brazil	3.01	-6
China	1.41	-56
Egypt	2.82	-50
Iceland	7.44	+131
Poland	2.29	-29
Sweden	4.59	+43
Thailand	1.78	-45
Ukraine	1.71	-47

Source: The Economist, 2/1/07

It doesn't appear that anybody has started a company by purchasing massive amounts of Big Macs and shipping them to Iceland to take advantage of the big difference in selling prices. Presumably McDonald's fish sandwich is cheaper in Iceland, where fish are many and cattle are few. The index, however, is an interesting rough indicator of what currencies may be overvalued and undervalued. Of course, to the layman, the table suggests a dartboard might have more predictive power than the theory of purchasing power parity, at least with hamburgers.

In a Relative Way

A more accurate way of comparing exchange rates is to compare an array of goods from country to country, called *relative purchasing power parity*. This permits economists to look at how price levels and the rate they are changing in different countries affect price levels.

As with single goods, the theory doesn't work out perfectly in practice, but with a broader sample of goods being compared, relative purchasing power is a more accurate predictor in the long run.

EconoTalk

The theory of **relative purchasing power parity** says that changes in national price levels determine increases and decreases in exchange rates in the long run.

Exchange Rates in the Short Run

In previous sections, we looked at how fundamental economic indicators influence exchange rates in the long run. From now until then, however, changes—sometimes sudden, large changes—in exchange rates occur for other reasons.

Where the Real Money Is

Despite all the attention paid to currency involved in the global trade of goods and services, only about 2 percent of the total foreign exchange transactions are devoted to it. The bulk of the trade in foreign exchange involves stocks, bonds, property, and treasury securities. With buying and selling of these assets going on around the clock and around the world, transactions occur fast and can have sudden impacts. And critics charge that a full 80 percent of world currency transactions are made by people speculating on future currency values. Speculators, though, serve an important role in allowing firms that don't wish to speculate on future currency values to lock in future currency values today.

Boiling short-term fluctuations down to two things might sound pretty simplistic, but bear in mind that in a huge market there is lots of room for interpretation. Let's start with one of the factors and get a closer look.

Interest in the Rates

Investors looking for the best deal seek out rates of return that are both high and reliable. This, of course, can be a difficult combination to achieve, but there's nothing wrong with trying. When the rates of return are relatively high for a country's assets, investors worldwide will want to invest and will need to buy that county's currency to do so, which drives up the exchange rates. If the rates of return are low in comparison to other alternatives, less of their money is purchased and the light demand leads to depreciation of the currency.

Nominal and Real Interest Rates

When it comes to exchange rates, the *nominal interest rate* is a weighted average of the rates between one country and its major trading partners. The "weight" assigned to each partner depends on how large a percentage of total trade it accounts for.

EconoTalk

Nominal interest rates are the stated rates for financial assets.

Probably the best-known tracker of nominal rates over time is the "Major Currency Index," published by the Federal Reserve. It shows the weighted average change in the American dollar's value relative to the currencies of its seven largest trading partners. A year when the index rises means the dollar has appreciated against the other currencies, and a year when it falls mean it has depreciated. Following are some selected years from the Federal Reserve's Index; 1973 serves as the base year.

Select Years Exchange Rates for the American Dollar

Year	Nominal Rate	Real Rate
1973	100	100
1982	116.2	109
1986	112	99.2
1990	89.1	84.7
1996	87.4	85.3
2003	88.6	94.6

EconoTalk

Real interest rates are calculated by starting with the nominal rate and subtracting inflation.

Strictly interpreted, the nominal rate is not your real return, because inflation (a loss of purchasing power) eats away at it. For example, if you invested in a financial asset with an 8 percent interest rate but inflation is running at 3 percent, that loss of money's value cuts into your earnings. For a nation, the *real interest rate* comes from the weighted average nominal rate minus the rise in general price levels.

For Better or Worse: Expectations of Exchange

Currency speculators make predictions about the future and use these to inform their choices. A high interest rate is generally attractive, but loses its luster if raging inflation is seen on the horizon. Lower rates may not look so good at first, but an expected minimal inflation creep dresses it up a bit.

Expectations for the future change constantly. New information becomes available and is incorporated into predictions. Maybe that country with the favorable rate of exchange suddenly looks unstable politically—which changes the outlook considerably. Or maybe a developing nation whose currency hasn't been regarded too favorably is experiencing a surprisingly healthy economic growth and is therefore "promoted" to a higher tier.

Speculating on Money Movements

For those able to predict the direction of exchange rates, there is lots of money—of all denominations—to be made. The same holds true for those alert to differences in currency valuations that can be translated into profits.

What benefit do currency speculators bring to world trade? For one thing, many businesses prefer to avoid the risk of shifting currency values. A company considering investing millions to expand production of a product for sale overseas may wish to lock in today's exchange rate. Their new products may not be ready to sell for a year, and since no one can know what exchange rates will be then, they will want to reduce their exposure to adverse exchange rates. Businesses that don't want to speculate on future exchange rates can contract with currency speculators who do.

As we have seen with exchange rates, they aren't as equal in all places as theories with an array of simplifying assumptions (necessary for theories to have value) make it sound. What that means is that a currency is selling for less in one country than it is in another. A smart speculator can profit by buying it in the cheaper location and selling it in the pricier market.

Another good strategy (for those good at reading the exchange rate tea leaves) is to buy rights to purchase currencies at future prices for hopefully less than what they will be selling them for.

The Least You Need to Know

◆ With no intrinsic value, the exchange rates of the world's major currencies are determined by supply and demand.

◆ The determinants of supply and demand are mostly fundamental economic factors such as productivity, trade policy, and price levels.

◆ An appreciating currency sounds good, but it comes with the downside of less-competitive exports and vulnerabilities to competing imports.

◆ A depreciating currency sounds bad, but it comes with the upside of exports priced more attractively abroad and domestic goods that are more competitive with imports.

Chapter 15

Money Management and Currencies in Crisis

In This Chapter

- ◆ Fixed exchange versus floating exchange: which is better?
- ◆ Controlling the float: target exchange rates
- ◆ The affect of national crises on currency

Our previous looks at how exchanges rates are determined may make it sound as though all countries handle their currencies in pretty much the same way. But despite common factors that are necessary to have a healthy monetary system, there are alternative exchange rate systems available. In this chapter, we look at those alternatives and the strengths and weaknesses that come with them.

There's More Than One Way to Skin a Currency

The big decision countries have to make about their currencies is whether to let free-market forces determine the rate of exchange or whether to set and manage it themselves. Member countries of the International Monetary Fund can follow any exchange rate system they want, as long as it meets three conditions:

1. Exchange rates are not to be manipulated to gain unfairly from adjustments in the balance of payments.

2. Short-run turmoil in exchange rates should be addressed by member countries.

3. The interests of other members should be kept in mind when countries enter exchange markets.

To Fix or to Float, That Is the Question

The broad choice is between a *fixed exchange rate* and a *floating exchange rate*. To provide insight into which system is right for different kinds of countries, the International Monetary Fund (IMF) published a general guide. The following sections address a few parts from that guide.

Choosing an Exchange Rate System

The "gold standard" fixed currency values to a fixed weight of gold, and thus world currencies were exchanged at rates fixed to each other. After going off the gold standard, fixed exchange rates were tried for a while but then replaced with floating rates.

EconoTalk

A **fixed exchange rate** is usually tied to a major currency, such as the American dollar.

A **floating exchange rate** is determined by the free market forces of supply and demand.

Fixed exchange rates may be best when …

◆ A large percent of what a nation produces is traded to other countries. As a result, currency fluctuations can be expensive, especially for small, open economies.

◆ A developing country has "young" (and small) financial markets where a few foreign exchange transactions could cause significant upward or downward movement.

◆ The central bank is very new or has a poor reputation, which means the confidence of a fixed rate is important.

Floating exchange rates may be best when …

◆ A country has high inflation, which means a fixed rate could make their goods uncompetitive in foreign markets.

◆ Wages are inflexible.

◆ A country has a large, stable economy and is open to international trade and capital.

Source: International Monetary Fund

Holding On to a Steady Hand

Of the 187 members of the International Monetary Fund, only 35 use floating exchange rates for their currency. Forty-one (see the following table) don't use their own currency at all; they use another country's or share a currency with a group of countries. Forty-three have fixed exchanged rates, and 47 have managed floating rate systems—meaning they only let the forces of supply and demand have so much say.

What exchange rate systems are used? This list shows how many countries use each system:

System	Number of IMF Member Countries
No separate currency	41
Currency board arrangements	7
Fixed exchange rates	43
Pegged rates within bands	4
Crawling pegged rates	5
Rates within crawling bands	5
Managed floating exchange rates	47
Floating exchange rates	35

Source: International Monetary Fund

Why Not Go It Alone?

What it comes down to is that the world's currency systems are dominated by a few currencies from the major economies. These countries buy and sell so much around the world, and are so large, that they will dominate whether smaller countries use their own money or not.

For a small country selling to the big dogs, it can make sense to simply tie its money's value to the larger country. Plus, the big country is probably already exerting a lot of control over prices. Not only that, a developing country trying to establish itself as financially responsible can signal that intent by pegging its money to a stable economy, a strategy that won't work if they mismanage their money supply.

If you want a clear picture of currency domination, look at the makeup of foreign exchange holdings in the following table (proportion of a particular country's currency):

Percent a Country's Currency in World Foreign Reserves

Currency	Percent
American Dollar	64.8
Japanese Yen	4.5
Pound Sterling	4.4
Swiss Franc	.7
Euro	14.6
Other	11.0
Total	100.0

Source: International Monetary Fund

More on Fixed Exchange Rates

Exchange rates completely determined by supply and demand (and the underlying factors that determine them) are something only a handful of countries have been willing to go with. Prior to the 1970s, when what was left of the gold standard was abandoned, most countries used fixed exchange rates between different countries. Changes in the fixed rate came from central banks/monetary authorities when long-run trends made them necessary.

Official Exchange

When currencies were backed by gold, fixed rates were simple. When 35 American dollars could buy an ounce of gold and 12.5 British pounds could also buy an ounce of gold, it was easy to calculate that it took $2.80 to get 1 pound. Even now the idea is the same in that you can fix, say, 3 units of a country's currency to $1, but there is nothing with independent market value standing behind any of the paper.

EconoTalk

In a fixed-rate system, nations give their currency a **par value**; which is a statement of the money's value in terms of something else, such as gold or another currency.

It is common for developing countries to set their *par value* in units of one of the major currencies. Then they establish, or "defend," their currency by buying and selling its new currency for the major currency at the same rate. So if Country A fixes its money at $2 for $1 of Country B, and $1 of Country B money is worth $3 of Country C, it is also possible to exchange $2 from Country A for $6 of Country C.

The Stabilizers

After a new currency has been established at a fixed rate, the issuing country wants to maintain it. They do this by establishing an exchange stabilization fund and spending from it to keep the exchange rate from straying too far away from the *official exchange rate*. Has the exchange rate gone up too high? Then sell funds to increase the supply and drive down the price. Has the exchange rate dropped too low? Then buy enough of it to raise that equilibrium rate.

EconoTalk

The **official exchange rate** is calculated by comparing the par values of two currencies.

Taking a Dive: Forced Devaluation

What happens when the fixed exchange rate chosen by a central bank differs from the market price? The answer shows up in the balance of payments. If the fixed rate is too high, citizen consumers take advantage of the money's extra buying power relative to other currencies and buy more foreign goods than they sell to foreigners. These increased imports and reduced exports show up as deficits in the balance of payments.

A challenge with *devaluation* is keeping it secret from speculators, who, should they catch a whiff of an upcoming devaluation, will immediately sell the soon-to-be-devalued currency. If the desire to devalue is obvious to a particular nation, why wouldn't it be to profit-motivated speculators?

EconoTalk

A currency **devaluation** is done to offset a balance of payments deficit by reducing the value of a nation's currency.

Of course, it is hard to keep politics and special interests separate from currency management. Domestic manufacturers often push for weaker currency to make their products more competitive at home and overseas. And since devaluation of currency can be achieved by printing more, government officials and politically connected businesses are often eager to help with the spending spree.

Other countries may not be enthusiastic about a devaluation, but for now the cheaper currency makes that country's goods more attractive, and somebody else is going to lose sales. Speaking of product prices, make sure you know the difference between depreciation and devaluation, for they are different things—though both result in a lower exchange rate.

Did You Know? _____

A depreciation in currency reflects a drop in value as determined by the market and is volatile. A devaluation of a currency means that a new, official and lower, fixed rate is being set.

A currency appreciation reflects a rise in value as determined by the market and is volatile. A revaluation of a currency means that a new, official, and higher fixed rate is being set.

Liftoff: Forced Revaluation

Sometimes the opposite of the previous statement occurs—a nation's currency drops in value so that there is a surplus, or a predicted surplus, in the balance of payments. In this case, a country, at low relative prices, is able to sell plenty to other countries, and imports have difficulty competing when they enter the country.

EconoTalk _____

A currency **revaluation** happens to offset a balance of payment's surplus by increasing the value of a nation's currency.

If word of a *revaluation* got out, speculators would rush in to buy the currency, so as with a devaluation, nations play their plans close to the vest. After a new exchange rate is set, say going from $1 of Country X's money being equal to $2 of Country Y's to $1.50 of X's equaling $2 of Y, Country X will enter the exchange market and buy and sell to support the change.

Floating Exchange Rates

An alternative to setting par and official rates of exchange is a floating exchange rate. A floating exchange rate is flexible, meaning that it will be set every day, and probably change many times a day, in the foreign exchange market. A true floating rate means a country is allowing the free market to set its money's value. The free market's point of view, of course, is not always in line with how a nation wants to be seen.

Cruising to Equilibrium

Under a floating system, the exchange rate is the same thing as the equilibrium point set by supply and demand in the foreign exchange market. Over time, deficits and surpluses in the balance of payments will be corrected by changes in the floating rate.

Rates and Restrictions

One surprising consequence of floating rates is that they adjust to changes in economic policy. For example, let's say a domestic manufacturer of dishwashers is worried about losing jobs to foreign competition and convinces the government to restrict the importation of dishwashers. With purchases of foreign dishwashers decreasing, less foreign currency is being purchased. The foreign currency, responding to a decrease in demand, declines in value. This makes its country's goods cheaper in the dishwasher manufacturer's country. As a result, foreign sales of other goods go up, which causes revenue and jobs to be lost. In other words, in a floating system, it's hard to make interfering with the economy pay off, except to the special interests that push for intervention.

To Float or Not to Float

The big advantage of a floating rate is its simplicity. The exchange rate is sensitive to changes in supply and demand and adjusts quickly. Further, without the rules and administration that come with fixed rates, the process works efficiently.

On the other hand, a floating rate can be prone to big swings in value, which could scare off investors and traders. These risks are compounded when governments pursue policies (such as severe trade restrictions) that amplify them.

Target Exchange Rates

To avoid wild fluctuations, many governments don't allow for a "full" float and instead try to keep the exchange rate at a point, or within a range, they are comfortable with.

When conditions, policies, or economic goals change, the *target exchange rate* can be changed. Maintaining a target rate in reality, though, can be difficult, especially when it conflicts with what the free market would set as an equilibrium point itself.

 EconoTalk

A **target exchange rate** is what governments enter the exchange market to achieve or maintain under a managed float system.

Short-Run Float Direction

A managed float system usually focuses on exchange rates in the short run, which is where the big, sudden ups and downs occur.

Here the challenge is to respond quickly and effectively. This is a market, after all, where speculators with profit motives and quick access to information move fast. A slow-acting government may not arrive in the market until the problem has passed, or gone on to the next step and become a crisis.

Long-Run Float Direction

In the long run, if a country intends to keep a floating rate and not switch to a full fixed rate, the market will decide what a currency's value is. The reason for this is that, though extreme swings that aren't always sensible occur in the short run, over time markets make efficient use of all available information and determine the best valuation.

Policies for Stability

Central banks step in to try and reach the ultimate goal, which is currency stability. The tools of central banks sound simple and easy to wield, but using them effectively means interpreting whatever information is available wisely and generating good ideas of what the economic future may hold—not an easy thing to do. This difficulty would be compounded if central banks were run by politicians or vested interests, and this is why most of those from the major economies are independent or, at least, have a significant degree of unencumbered decision-making power.

Did You Know? _____

If a currency is appreciating and the central bank wants to counter it, they will follow an expansionary monetary policy (increase the money supply).

If a currency is depreciating and the central bank wants to counter it, they will follow a monetary policy of contraction (decrease the money supply).

In Crawls the Peg

Instead of going for a fixed or floating rate, some countries choose a middle ground. What they do is make many small changes to the par value to offset any deficits or surpluses in the balance of payments. The advantage of this approach is that small changes mean the harm done by a bad choice is limited and, when made in the right direction, change is gradual instead of sudden and destabilizing.

A *crawling peg* is popular with countries experiencing significant inflations or other rapidly changing economic conditions. Adjustments in currency can be made frequently and quickly, with the twin goals of responding to frequent alterations in the environment and avoiding sudden, large adjustments.

 EconoTalk

A **crawling peg** is a cross between a floating rate and a fixed rate.

When Crisis Visits Currencies

The downside of an international monetary system is that currencies can be thrown into crisis by changes in the market climate. Crisis conditions don't normally strike the major, developed economies, but are experienced in smaller economies whose exchange rates are tied to the "big boys" or whose economies are heavily dependent on trade with them.

You've heard the expression, "a rising tide lifts all boats." When it comes to currencies, a small ship tied to an ocean liner can be sunk by a wave that a big boat was only sprayed by.

In any country, large or small, access to the printing press tempts politicians and special interests. It is easy to be overly optimistic about the quantities of currency governments can print and spend without igniting inflation and currency crises. Ocean liners can disrupt small boats, but far more small boats sink from internal leaks.

In the international market, a currency crisis is usually precipitated by the decisions of speculators. Simply put, if they view a currency as being unstable or unworthy of investment, its value plummets. It's easy to blame speculators, then, for a currency crisis, especially when there are big players from rich countries, but usually there are good reasons for what they do. Speculators are out to make a profit, not destroy currencies. Mostly speculators are responding to economic indicators, and when these indicators (productivity, inflation, trade policies) start giving off troubling signals, speculators tend to move in quickly.

The Least You Need to Know

◆ Alternative currency systems range from allowing forces of supply and demand to determine rates of exchange to governments setting exchange rates themselves and acting to maintain them.

- No matter how much a nation tries to manage its currency, they cannot ignore the international currency market if they want to trade with the rest of the world.

- Short-term swings in exchange rates can be volatile, but in the long run the market moves to a sensible rate.

- The disadvantage of an enormous, interlinked system of international exchange is that currencies of small and developing economies can be thrown into crisis.

Part  5

The Territories Less Explored

The growing global economy of the last few decades has brought modest but significant economic and health gains to billions, thanks mostly to economic reforms in China and India, the world's two most populated countries. Left behind, though, are at least a billion more people in Africa and Latin America, as well as hundreds of millions still desperately poor in India, China, Indonesia, and many other countries. The countries that have prospered have done so by increasing economic freedom for their own people, and by opening their economies to outside investment and expertise.

This part explores how economic freedom can bring wealth to a nation. We also take a look at global warming, terrorism, dumping, and quality-of-life issues.

"I hear it's going to be a Starbucks."

Chapter 16

Friends in Need

In This Chapter

- ◆ Does foreign aid create dependence?
- ◆ Distributing foreign aid—the risk of misspent funds
- ◆ Major public and private donors to developing countries

In April 2006, BBC News posted a story about firewood collectors in Ethiopia. These are females, from childhood to old age, who travel outside the city of Addis Ababa in search of firewood and spend a full day collecting and carrying a single load back to the city, where they can sell it for a couple dollars. The BBC story quoted a 10-year-old girl saying, "I don't want to have to carry wood all my life. But at the moment I have no choice because we are so poor. All of us children carry wood to help our mother and father buy food for us. I would prefer to be able to just go to school and not worry about getting money."

Whatever the advantages of global economic interactions, there remain countries where poverty is the norm, economies do not grow, and living standards do not improve. Over decades, many hundreds of billions of foreign aid dollars have flowed into underdeveloped countries whose citizens have seen little if any improvement. Is aid then just a cynical ploy to funnel money through destitute countries on the way to corporate coffers? Is development aid poorly conceived and doomed to fail? Is it impossible to effectively help? Or have we not done enough of what really works?

Does Foreign Aid Help or Hurt?

Providing real help to poor people in *developing countries* does not have to cost a lot. Medicine to prevent malaria is less than 15 cents a dose; providing new mothers with the care necessary to dramatically reduce the infant mortality rate is just a few dollars per mother; building schools in poverty-stricken regions and educating children is surprisingly inexpensive. So why aren't the world's wealthy rushing to help out? Though not to the degree some of us might want, many have been.

Since the mid-1950s, western governments have spent more than $2.3 trillion on foreign aid, yet even the inexpensive measures just outlined have not been carried out to a significant degree. Aid to Africa alone is almost $570 billion, but most African countries are little better off than they were in the 1960s. But foreign aid funds usually came from donor countries with strings attached, often tying grants to specific roads, dams, bridges, factories, or other projects. Apart from mismanagement and corruption have been broader questions of whether many aid projects made economic sense in the first place. Roads and dams have been built in the wrong places, and dozens of costly factories dropped into developing countries could not survive without supporting industry. Development projects that looked good on paper (though apparently not good enough to attract private investment) have turned out to be costly white elephants scattered across the underdeveloped world.

EconoTalk

Developing countries are seen as those with few capital goods, a lack of modern technology, poor health care, growing populations, and high rates of illiteracy and unemployment, with agriculturally based economies.

The Helping Hand Reflex

In wealthy industrial countries where jobs and food are plentiful and whatever we need is usually no more than a shopping mall away, it is natural to assume that simply providing money to the poverty-stricken will enable them to buy what they need to survive and make the necessary investments to grow a healthy economy.

But it is worth considering that none of today's prosperous countries became wealthy through foreign aid. Careless donations can have disturbing consequences. Just as we would be wary of giving money to an alcoholic, giving billions to government officials in poor countries distorts their incentives and distracts them from providing traditional government services.

Crippling by Kindness?

In the 1960s, Indian economist Jagdish Bhagwati pleaded with the United States to cease donating huge shipments of wheat to his home country. At first this sounds insane—a plea to stop feeding hungry people? But that wasn't what he meant; of course shipments of food would be gratefully accepted in times of famine. The problem was the constant inflow of food from outside.

He believed that this free or low-cost wheat made India dependent and hindered their ability to feed themselves. Gradually American wheat shipments to India fell off, and gradually India's domestic production of wheat increased. Not only do they now produce enough wheat for themselves, they also export it to other countries.

Inflows of donated food and money to poor countries have yielded little lasting benefit and instead resulted in large debt burdens for developing economies. The current movement to forgive the debts of poor countries makes sense: by cutting down or eliminating debt, these countries then have more resources available to help their citizens. On the other hand, will forgiving debt lead to more borrowing by officials who believe the money never has to be paid back, or that relief is always available should they fall behind on repayments?

Did You Know?

Top-down economic planning tries to coordinate economic activity with directives from government ministries or corporate headquarters. Market organization is more spontaneous and coordinates economic activity from the bottom up, as people and firms respond to changing prices. Market organization has significant advantages in coordinating the economic plans of millions in both modern and underdeveloped economies.

A Friend in Deed

Though infusions of cash, medicine, and expertise can be helpful to poor countries, long-term improvements seem to depend more on changes in economic institutions. As Chapter 18, concerning economic freedom, tells us, simply allowing businesses and individuals to use their resources to develop enterprises while governments protect property and enforce contracts can make an enormous difference. Countries such as South Korea and Estonia are wonderful examples of what can be accomplished with a simple set of economic reforms.

One example of a homegrown program that stressed accountability and innovation was launched in Mexico in 1997. PROGRESA (Education, Health, and Food Plan of

Mexico) gives cash grants to mothers, but only if they keep their children in school and participate in health-care programs. Though the Mexican government lacks the money to do this with everybody who would benefit, the results of this relatively small-scale effort were impressive: the children stayed in school longer, were better educated, and suffered less illness. In addition, healthier, better-educated children are more likely to be healthier, wealthier adults who are able to pass on these kinds of benefits to the next generation.

Since the initial success of PROGRESA, its budget and scope have grown in Mexico, and the World Bank has launched similar programs in other countries.

Fishing Lessons

The key to effective aid may lie in creating approaches where citizens of poor countries take ownership of projects and have incentives to make them work.

For example, Population Services International is a group seeking to reduce the ravages of malaria in Africa. The country of Malawi tried a novel approach. Already employing a lot of local staff, they directed them to identify those in high-risk groups, mostly pregnant women and children younger than five years old. They sold mosquito nets at deeply discounted prices to mothers visiting clinics for health care. Local nurses, not outsiders, would explain the benefits of the nets to the mothers and received a small commission for each set of netting sold. The mothers were more inclined to follow the advice of local nurses and the nurses themselves, whose salaries were small, were motivated both by the chance to provide better health care and the opportunity to supplement their meager incomes. This approach was so successful, it is now being mirrored in other countries facing similar challenges.

Into the Wrong Hands

A huge problem has always been getting foreign aid into the hands of the people who will distribute it efficiently and fairly, which is harder than it sounds. Aid money may be shifted to bribes and private bank accounts instead. Shipments of food can be sold for cash that is then used to buy weapons. The result can be that foreign aid is hijacked and financing the further deterioration of already harsh living conditions.

When Robin Gives to the Hoods

In the following table, we see countries ranked, with #1 being the most honest, according to the level of corruption that exists in each government. Where more than one country inhabits a rank, it means they are tied. Note that the most corrupt countries also tend to be among the world's poorest.

Index of Corruption for Selected Countries (2006)

Country	Rank
Finland, Iceland, New Zealand	1
Denmark	4
Singapore	5
Sweden	6
Switzerland	7
United States	20
Italy	45
Turkey	60
Brazil, India	40
Nigeria	142
Bangladesh, Chad, Congo, Sudan	156
Iraq, Guinea, Myanmar	160
Haiti	163

Source: Transparency International

In general, the poorest countries have the least free, most corrupt, and most violent governments. The challenge, then, is to help people trapped in parts of the world where helping hands are often turned away. And of course, people shouldn't be trapped in such countries in the first place. People unable to vote for a better government should at least have the option to "vote" with their feet and relocate to better-governed lands.

Financing Development

Along with national governments, there are other agencies, organizations, and individuals involved in providing aid to the developing world. A few of the major players are described in the following sections.

The World Bank

The World Bank is a constellation of five organizations that came into being in 1945. Its purpose has shifted over the years, and it now provides financing and advice with the goals of promoting economic development and reducing poverty.

The five organizations that make up the World Bank are:

1. International Bank for Reconstruction and Development

2. International Development Association

3. International Finance Corporation

4. Multilateral Investment Guarantee Group

5. International Center for Settlement of Investment Disputes

Having had trouble demonstrating the efficacy of its earlier efforts, the World Bank in recent years has become much more concerned with documenting results and utilizing more "homegrown" approaches.

International Monetary Fund

The International Monetary Fund (IMF) is made up of 185 member countries. Its purpose, which has also shifted as the international monetary system has changed, is to facilitate monetary cooperation, financial stability, trade, economic growth, and poverty reduction around the world. How's that for a tall order?

The ravages of the Great Depression provided the impetus for the IMF, which was founded in 1947 when the original 29 member countries agreed to its charter. The IMF mostly provides assistance to countries that are experiencing problems with their balance of payments. This help comes in the form of loans and advice. Countries receiving this assistance are usually required to enact a series of reforms designed by the IMF, with the goal of keeping them out of similar kinds of trouble in the future. As economic theories have changed over the years, economic advice and reform proposals have evolved. In retrospect, it is not clear whether past IMF reforms pushed on developing countries were actually helpful.

When the Sharks Lie Down with the Guppies

From small local organizations to huge global banks, interest has been growing in micro loans, which are small loans (up to a few hundred dollars) made to poor individuals and businesses without the credit history, collateral, or track record to secure a traditional loan.

The micro loans movement started as a mostly nonprofit venture because these small loans cost much more, per dollar loaned, than larger loans. As large banks have joined in, however, with their ability to "bundle" loans and access huge pools of money, these little loans can add up to large returns.

The first bank listed in the following table, Compartamos in Mexico, made more than 600,000 micro loans in 2007, and has a history of being profitable. In 2005, the microfinance lent $7.3 billion, a significant rise from $4.9 billion in 2003.

Top Returning Microfinance Institutions (2004)

Institution	Percent Return on Equity
Compartamos	48
CMAC Trujillo	35
CMAC Cusco	33
CMAC Arequipa	32
Emprendamos	29
WWB Cali	27
Confia	26

Source: MicroRate

Givers and NGOs

Nongovernmental organizations (NGO) are set up for specific purposes that may be very similar to what governments do but operate without the same restrictions or standards. These organizations range from the American Association of Retired Persons to Human Rights Watch to Oxfam. Much as with governments, NGOs involved in providing foreign aid have increased their emphasis on results that can be measured and practical approaches that rely, whenever possible, on the talents of local citizens.

Private Philanthropy

Translated from the nineteenth century into 2005 dollars, John D. Rockefeller gave away $6 billion. That's a lot of money in any day, but it pales next to the total given away by the all-time champion of charitable giving, Bill Gates, who has already donated more than $31 billion and is expected to give away even more than that in the years ahead.

And it's not just individuals giving away money on their own. Bill Gates set up his own charitable foundation, and the number of charitable foundations in America has risen from approximately 22,000 in 1982 to more than 65,000 today.

Top 10 American Givers (Donations Made from 2001 to 2005)

Name	Donation (in Billions of Dollars)
Gordon and Betty Moore	7.05
Bill and Melinda Gates	5.46
Warren Buffet	2.62
George Soros	2.37
Eli and Edythe Broad	1.48
James and Virginia Stowers	1.21
Walton Family	1.10
Alfred Mann	.99
Michael and Susan Dell	.93
George Kaiser	.62

Source: Business Week

Much of the "new money" involved in philanthropy today comes from high-tech entrepreneurs who are younger and more actively involved in giving than were the industrialists of the late nineteenth century. This is reflected in their insistence on knowing where their money is going and how it is being allocated. Similar to analyzing the results of a for-profit firm, the new philanthropists want a "bang for the buck" that can be clearly seen, felt, and heard.

The Least You Need to Know

◆ Simply giving money to a poor country does not help in and of itself and may unknowingly finance corrupt dealings.

◆ For both government and private agencies, there has been a heightened emphasis on results that can be measured, evaluated, and, when good, repeated in other places.

◆ Private philanthropy has grown to a level never before seen, even in the "golden age" of huge donations of the nineteenth-century industrialists.

Threats to Global Growth

In This Chapter

- ◆ Equality is not the goal of globalization
- ◆ Limiting pollution and the tragedy of the commons
- ◆ International conflicts and the role of terrorism in the global economy
- ◆ Isolationism: the road to poverty

Economics teaches us that everything comes with costs, no matter how desirable or worthwhile particular goals and achievements are. The process of economic globalization has brought a multitude of benefits to countries around the world, but they are not free. Creating goods uses resources and creates waste that has to be disposed of. Sometimes development costs are steep and raise the question of whether globalization is worth the expense. The disadvantages include environmental damage, pollution, income inequality, and cultural losses and homogenization.

Economics encourages activities up to the point where the additional (marginal) benefits equal the additional costs—beyond this point, the costs exceed the benefits. But there is widespread disagreement about globalization's tradeoffs and how they're measured (not everything can be put into dollars). This chapter takes a look at the different views on globalization.

Not Everybody Wants the World to Be Flat

Differences in the resources and abilities of individuals, firms, and countries, are what makes trade beneficial. There is a fear that falling barriers of geography, technology, and politics will make the entire world one vast, homogeneous marketplace where all goods, services, and incomes are similar, and no matter where you go, everything will look the same.

Quality vs. Quantity

Measures such as GDP are good at showing economic output, but cannot show how people are doing in a broader sense. If an economy grows by, say, 10 percent, does that mean its citizens are 10 percent happier? Will the uptick in wealth today cause lost wealth and happiness in the future? Or was this 10 percent gain in material wealth (the stuff GDP measures) bought at the expense of unmeasured pleasures like a scenic view, quiet neighborhood, hiking trail, or roadside forest? Economics teaches us that wants are unlimited; when one want is satisfied, people move on to the next. What if your higher income brings large amounts of stress, so that with more of "life's good things" you discover that you still lack what you want, no matter how much has been achieved, and now have less time and are more tired and worried to boot?

Is it possible to simply learn how to appreciate fewer material things more, thereby increasing your satisfaction at lower cost? As the Chinese proverb says, "He is richest whose pleasures are cheapest." Many religions and systems of belief agree, but economics, grounded as it is in the measurable and objective, doesn't provide us with an easy road map for this.

It's not that economists, or the discipline of economics itself, don't care about quality of life. On the contrary, from Adam Smith to economists of the present day, it is broadly acknowledged that happiness and personal satisfaction are the proper goals of economic activity—it's just that economics lets individuals work out precisely what that is for themselves.

Problems occur when inhabitants of a world constrained by limited resources value these resources differently and disagree about who has the right to do what with them. A forest owner may think of trees as his crop to harvest, but neighbors likely think of the forest as beautiful scenery (while animals think of it as home). As more and more people are able to reach across the world to influence how resources are used (or abused), it is only natural that the clashes should become more pronounced.

Who Let the Culture Out?

Rates of obesity and diabetes have increased in Japan as western foods (especially in the form of fast food) have become more popular. Native languages and customs are ignored in recently developed areas where television and the Internet have been introduced (though the Internet also allows a worldwide following for obscure and endangered languages). Previously thriving small-town centers in the United States look like ghost towns after shop owners who cannot compete with the big chain stores shut down their stores. Local coffee shops are not able to go bean-to-bean with the new place that just opened across the street and is part of a chain that circles the globe.

Globalization is accused of homogenizing culture, but that also includes bringing a wondrous array of international culture and cuisine to American cities and suburbs. Before Starbucks brought European-style coffee shops to middle America, lattés were little known outside New York, San Francisco, and other big cities. Still, the question raised more and more often is this: Did the old and familiar have more value than we realized, and is it now too late to get it back?

When consumers choose Walgreens, Wal-Marts, and Big Box stores, they make smaller local stores fade away. Are individuals and groups less rational decision-makers because they frequently depend on incomplete or faulty information? If so, do we then need some kind of social "guardians" to preserve worthy traditions and institutions?

Somebody to Look Down On

When we judge how well off we are, we usually compare ourselves to those around us. It can be satisfying to have our income go up 20 percent when everybody else's goes up just 5 percent. At the same time, if our income goes up 20 percent and everybody else's also does, we may feel we are just keeping up. When our income remains the same and those around us get raises, we may feel worse off, even though things haven't really changed for us. Somehow we feel we've missed the boat and fallen behind.

It's not just money where this matters. People tend to cherish traditions and want to maintain the habits and customs they have grown accustomed to. Scandinavians serve their lutefisk at holidays, and though this barely preserved fish helped their ancestors survive long frozen winters, it is served today for cultural more than survival reasons (though surviving a serving of lutefisk is itself a challenge). America, with its long tradition of immigration, has mixed cultural traditions for over three centuries. Still, each time immigration patterns change, everyday Americans find themselves living and working next door to cultural traditions that seem weird even when compared to the Scandinavians and their lutefisk. Change is seen as something unwarranted, and naturally society wants to adhere to the "old ways."

Who Cleans Up the Mess?

Everybody likes a party, but nobody likes to clean up afterward. When it comes to economic globalization, a developing world where living standards are slowly rising for billions of people also means that vastly more oil and coal are burned, with big increases in the pollution released into the air and water.

Problems arise when an individual, firm, or country produces a product but does not pay its full cost. How can this happen? Let's say your company makes refrigerators. You pay for the materials, labor, equipment, and whatever else it takes to get your wares in shape for customers. But say your factory releases pollutants into the air. You probably won't have to pay for those, at least not directly, so an external cost not borne by your firm has been created. Even though your firm does not pay, somebody will—by having to look through smog or breathe slightly dirtier air.

The Tragedy of the Commons

What if your family was on vacation at a lake and witnessed another family leaving trash behind from a picnic? If the surrounding land is publicly owned and the upkeep is paid for by the local government, the polluting family, assuming they get away with it, do not have to pay the cost of cleaning up after themselves: somebody else using somebody else's money has to.

EconoTalk

The **tragedy of the commons** occurs when commonly owned natural resources are destroyed, over-used, degraded, or neglected because no one has the authority to limit access and overuse of them.

The *tragedy of the commons* has existed since ancient times; as forests were cleared and water polluted near cities, pollution levels accelerated dramatically with industrialization and population growth. Firms benefit from the resources used but "leave behind" costs for those around them to bear.

No one wants to be downstream of the upstream polluter, and the upstream polluter sees river flow as a free rubbish disposal system—pour waste in, and minutes later they are out of sight downstream.

So why not have everyone pay for exactly the resources they use and exactly the cleanup costs they incur? You probably guessed it right away: it's hard to say exactly what those costs are, and harder to say who should pay them—and that's before we even think about getting them to pay those costs.

Pennies for Pollution

Eliminating all pollution would also eliminate economic growth. Pollution is a cost of development, but how do nations best influence or control tradeoffs between pollution abatement and economic growth? One approach, based on the insights offered by economics, is for limits (mandated by governments) to be set for pollution. Government and independent organizations try to establish the amount of wastes that can be released into the air and water without damaging the environment or imposing significant costs upon others. Individual firms are then allotted a share of pollution they may produce. If a firm is able to produce less, they can sell "rights to pollute" to firms desiring to emit more than their limit. The forces of supply and demand dictate what the rights sell for. Of course, deciding what environmental costs are "significant" is difficult, to say the least. It is clear that poisons from a factory that kill fish and endanger people should be stopped. But what about water that is just dirty and seems to disappear downstream? What about water that's clean but warm, so it raises the temperature of a river or stream and alters the ecosystem? What about smoke from backyard barbecues that some neighbors enjoy but others hate? Deciding who should have a right to do what when it comes to pollution is a complicated issue that communities deal with differently across the United States and around the world.

Did You Know? _____

The largest-scale program using market incentives to limit greenhouse gas emissions was created along with the Kyoto Protocol: the European Union Emission Trading Scheme, launched in January 2005. The scheme limits carbon dioxide emissions from power plants and large factories. These installations are able to buy and sell credits to pollute. A factory that emits less carbon dioxide than its cap can sell the difference as credits to other installations desiring to release more than their allotment. The first two years of the program saw high levels of compliance and established a market for carbon trading.

Setting up systems to control pollution of any kind is difficult. It's one thing for wealthy countries that are already economically developed to clean up their act, but another for countries of lesser means. Finding ways for countries to work together and limit damage done to the environment is a real challenge.

Countries took a step forward on this issue in 2005, when the Kyoto Protocol was launched. The primary goal of the protocol is to limit greenhouse gases around the globe. The result has been steadily increasing success in the limitation of harmful emissions from factories and power plants.

Clean Water vs. Running Water

In 1820, still early in the industrial revolution, the world's population stood at 1 billion. Today it is more than 6.6 billion. Two rapidly developing economic power-houses, China and India, have respective populations of 1.3 billion and 1.1 billion. As the earnings of their citizens rise, so do rates of car ownership and consumption in general. Additional pressure is put on limited resources such as oil, and with more people using more energy, the impact on the environment grows.

To date, mankind has been very efficient about getting more out of the natural resources at our disposal and bringing additional resources "online." The questions today are how much longer can we do this, and when will we exceed the earth's capacity to deal with the consequences?

Did You Know?

In his 1798 piece, *An Essay on the Principle of Population,* Thomas Malthus predicted, "The power of population is so superior to the power of the earth to produce subsistence for man, that premature death must in some shape or other visit the human race."

Did You Know?

Previously the International Energy Agency had predicted that China would surpass the United States as the world's top greenhouse gas producer in 2010. In May 2007, they revised their prediction so that China would achieve that distinction in 2010 and, given their rapid economic growth and dependence on coal, would also offset any reductions in greenhouse gas emissions made elsewhere.

In the next 25 years, if the current rate of increase continues, China's greenhouse gas emissions will be double those of the Organization for Economic Cooperation and Development, whose members include the United States, Europe, Canada, and Japan.

The good news for the world that comes with billions in China and India gradually integrating into the global economy, apart from the improving quality of life they will enjoy, is that people are producers as well as consumers. Many millions more people will decide to become research scientists, engineers, and entrepreneurs, and turn their intellectual energy toward tackling resource and environmental problems.

Instead of hundreds of millions planting rice by hand in China or struggling with plows and oxen in India, most will eventually join the ranks of productive workers and problem-solvers for the world economy.

Strategies for Sustainable Development

A popular principle in recent years is *sustainable development*. This refers to a balance between meeting needs and wants in the present while protecting the environment and not compromising the earth's quality for future generations. How's that for a tall order?

In prior centuries, there was little notion of sustainable development. The focus was simply on sustaining life itself and, when that was taken care of, using the resources at our disposal to improve living conditions. What sustainable development warns is that today's progress should not become tomorrow's burden.

Did You Know? _____

Plans are afoot to produce renewable diesel from animal fat. It takes an estimated 1 barrel of animal fat to produce one 42-gallon barrel of diesel.

A Savage Place

Though technology has developed at an exponential rate, and modern economies provide levels of goods and services unimaginable in the past, human nature itself has not changed. Suspicion of outsiders and the urge to fight about limited resources remain, whether they are necessary or not. Around the world, conflicts are predicted over limited resources, such as waters diverted from shared rivers, oil and gas deposits discovered where boundaries are disputed, and oil revenue sharing among ethnic groups within countries. And, of course, political, tribal, and ethnic conflict can erupt even without natural resource disputes.

The Challenge of Terror

In Chapter 1, we talked about how improvements in communications technology and the fall of transportation costs made it possible for global economic development to take off. What makes it possible for firms to do business almost anywhere, however, also makes it possible to do violence almost anywhere.

With modern media available, even small groups can make their presence felt in ways that were not possible even a few years ago. Larger groups with grievances and the organizational muscle to express them can dominate the news. The terrorist attacks of 9/11 showed us just how much harm a relatively small group can do, and how enormous the economic and psychological costs borne by the rest of the world are.

Terrorism's costs go beyond physical death and damage. For example, the Friday following the arrest of 172 Islamic militants accused of planning attacks on Saudi Arabian oil fields in April 2007, the price of crude oil jumped 2.2 percent, largely driven by fears of future attacks. Saudi Arabia provides 10 percent of the world's oil. Oil accounts for 45 percent of their Gross Domestic Product and 75 percent of government revenues. As you can see, terrorism is not just a social evil; it's also an economic nightmare.

Global Conflicts and Grudges

Countries actively engaged in economic relations with each other are much less likely to be involved in violent conflicts. Why fight when the benefits of mutually beneficial exchange are obvious? Old grudges and current conflicts, however, can interfere with the healthy exchange of resources.

It turns out that countries with the least economic freedom also have the most problems with violence and terrorism. The "opportunity cost" of violence and terrorism is less where young men lack opportunities for productive work. And even when work is available, some people prefer to nurse grudges. What do we do when the satisfactions gained by conflict in the present, or by pursuing a violent cause into the future, outweigh—for some groups—the benefits of peaceful participation in the global economy? Even if most countries can find ways to get along, not everybody will.

Did You Know?

When religious and political conflicts between countries rise, boycotting companies because of their nationality, not because of their goods or services, becomes more common. In market economies, people must pay a price to discriminate by not hiring or buying products from people they don't like.

Be they differences in religion, politics, ways of life, or disputes about boundaries, violent disagreements make the peaceable trade that characterizes economic development impossible. When economic development is impossible, the likely result is poverty and suffering, which only breeds more conflicts and encourages an ongoing negative cycle.

As the Gap Widens

Isolationism is a road to poverty—simply isolating ourselves from talents of others reduces the scope of trade and makes us pay too much to do everything ourselves.

Did You Know? _____

The European Commission predicts that, in 50 years, the European Union's GDP per person could be 8 percent higher from actively trading with China and India than would be the case if they didn't welcome their continued development. And if they don't embrace China and India? The result is a GDP per person that is 5 percent lower than what it could have been.

Income Inequality

As skills and education play a greater role in individual career success in an increasingly information-based economy, the gap widens between what those with the advanced skills earn and what everybody else earns. And earning is just part of the wealth picture. High savings rates enable wage-earners to become capitalists, as savings compound and investment income multiplies. Of course luck plays a role with investment returns, but high savings rates can transform national income as well as family income.

The Chinese are noted for high savings rates that average 40 percent, which is pretty amazing for a country with an average annual income of under $1,500 a year. How is it even possible? Well, for one thing, average income in China used to be much lower, and in 1985 is estimated to have been just $280. That is $280 annual, not monthly, income! (Most Chinese lived on farms growing much of their own food, so income figures are somewhat misleading.) So while annual incomes in China today seem low by American standards, they are much higher than what the average Chinese worker earned 20 years ago.

Hard work and high savings will propel Chinese workers to higher incomes, and job training and advanced education will also play a key role to increase worker productivity.

Could Today's Rich Be Tomorrow's Poor?

In the eighteenth century, China was the world's largest economy, with a Gross Domestic Product per person that was 700 percent of Britain's. But it had already set the stage for losing its dominant position. China refused to trade with the rest of the world and gave up the opportunity to benefit from the flood of global trade that followed the industrial revolution. When 1950 rolled around, China's GDP per person had declined 25 percent from where it had been late in the eighteenth century. Britain's had grown 500 percent.

It is a sign of a sea change in attitudes when citizens of the world's wealthy countries give as much attention to the threats posed to their well-being by emerging economies as they do to the poverty of these same places. Bear in mind, however, that between them, China and India still are home to more poor people than live in all of Africa.

Will the Pie Ever Be Big Enough?

In the nineteenth century, more economic progress and improvements in standards of living were made than in all prior centuries combined. In the twentieth century, once again, more progress was made than in all prior centuries combined—including the nineteenth.

Economic progress did not occur evenly, and there remain enormous differences between the rich and poor. Still, even in the world's wealthiest regions, new wants spring up as quickly as ever. Unlimited wants, coupled with only limited resources available to satisfy them, is basic to economics. It has only been in the last few hundred years that mankind could regularly meet even the basic needs of a portion of the world's population. Now, though still not for everybody, the basic wants of a large proportion of the world can be satisfied. But as these basic desires for food, shelter, and clothing are satisfied for more of the world's population, their attention turns to other goods, from basic electricity to refrigerators, air conditioners, televisions, and cars.

Always wanting things to be better and never being satisfied with the way things are has been and will continue to be a driving force for incredible progress.

The Least You Need to Know

◆ Human wants remain unlimited, even in wealthy nations, and scarcity remains a constant.

◆ The technology that makes global economic growth possible can also be used to do harm.

◆ As a cost of development, there is widespread disagreement on how much pollution is okay and how to manage it.

◆ Economics is good at measuring wealth in dollars but is not able to produce quality-of-life measures everybody can agree on.

Chapter 18

Free at Last

In This Chapter

- ◆ Measuring economic freedom
- ◆ The link between economic freedom and prosperity
- ◆ Freedom isn't just about making money

In recent years, it has become clear that the wealthiest, most successful economies are generally the freest. Their citizens enjoy the highest average incomes, the lowest rates of inflation, better health, and the greatest social stability. So why don't free markets abound in all the world's economies? The answers are complex, but it is worth noting that granting economic freedom to citizens requires removing economic power from the elites in government and politically connected companies. The richest man in the world, Carlos Slim, owns companies with monopoly control of Mexico's phone systems. More competition in Mexico's telecommunications markets would lower prices for everyday Mexicans, but hurt Mr. Slim's companies. A similar song plays in developing economies around the world.

Though resources will always be limited, open economies where contracts, property rights, and the rule of law are enforced encourage people to innovate and produce more and better goods and services. And when more and better goods and services are produced, there is more and better to consume.

Give Them What They Want

In *The Wealth of Nations*, Adam Smith explained why free economies provide prosperity for their citizens. The debate didn't end in 1776, however, in part because some gain so much from keeping the public confused about economic principles.

Adam Smith was far from an apologist for business, and in *The Wealth of Nations*, he is deeply critical of merchants and manufacturers: "People of the same trade seldom meet together, even for merriment and diversion, but the conversation ends in a conspiracy against the public, or in some contrivance to raise prices."

It is worth quoting Smith at length as he describes how the self-interest of merchants is often at odds with that of the people:

"Commerce, which ought naturally to be, among nations, as among individuals, a bond of union and friendship, has become the most fertile source of discord and animosity. The capricious ambition of kings and ministers has not, during the present and the preceding century, been more fatal to the repose of Europe than the impertinent jealousy of merchants and manufacturers. The violence and injustice of the rulers of mankind is an ancient evil, for which, I am afraid, the nature of human affairs can scarce admit of a remedy. But the mean rapacity, the monopolizing spirit of merchants and manufacturers, who neither are, nor ought to be, the rulers of mankind, though it cannot perhaps be corrected may very easily be prevented from disturbing the tranquility of anybody but themselves."

Merchants, Smith emphasized, promote economic regulations to protect themselves from competition. But economic freedom does not mean the opportunity to do whatever you want without limits. In fact, the full benefits of economic freedom can only be experienced in nations with strong, clear laws and institutions.

Beginning in 1996, an ongoing effort has been made to measure economic freedom and demonstrate its correlation to standards of living. The *Index of Economic Freedom* is the joint effort of The Heritage Foundation and *The Wall Street Journal*. It will not be the last word on the subject, of course, but its conclusions and methodology make it worth featuring as we near the end of this book.

Can Human Behavior Be Accounted For?

The challenge in measuring the impact of economic freedom is twofold: first you have to define what economic freedom is, and then you have to develop objective means of tracking it. Remember, we're talking human behavior here, a notoriously difficult thing to understand, predict, or manage. The following are the 10 measures of economic freedom, which will be defined in the passages that follow:

10 Indicators of Economic Freedom

1. Business freedom

2. Trade freedom

3. Fiscal freedom

4. Freedom from government

5. Monetary freedom

6. Investment freedom

7. Financial freedom

8. Property rights

9. Freedom from corruption

10. Labor freedom

Source: Index of Economic Freedom, *2007*

Business Freedom

The business freedom measure tells us how free citizens of a particular country are to start new businesses. It doesn't tell us merely whether they are allowed to or not, but incorporates things such as how difficult or easy it is to obtain permission to open or close a business. The easier it is to open a new business, the quicker new jobs and additional economic stimulation occur. Beyond that, in nations where it is difficult to start up a new enterprise, entrepreneurs may get discouraged and simply decide the grief isn't worth it.

Did You Know? _____

On average, worldwide, it takes 48 days to start up a new business. There is a wide range among countries, from 3 days in the United States to 92 days in India. When specific licenses are required, the average rises to 215 days. In some places, such as Ireland, it is a straightforward process and one knows approximately how long it will take. In other places, such as the Ukraine, a license may take years, with no guarantee the process will ever be completed.

Source: "Doing Business," World Bank, 2007

Trade Freedom

Countries earn a higher score for trade freedom with the fewer restrictions they place on imported goods, such as tariffs, quotas, and bureaucratic hurdles. Every country included in the *Index of Economic Freedom* restricts trade to some degree. Even those reluctant to impose tariffs and quotas will resort to other government-imposed restrictions.

Fiscal Freedom

Fiscal freedom examines what percentage of their incomes citizens from different countries must pay in taxes. Economically freer countries collect lower proportions of taxes and have lower tax rates than less free countries. The core question around taxation is, who is better suited to spend your earnings, you or the government? Though most support the need to collect taxes for the administration of basic public services (building roads, maintaining a military, and so on), beyond that nations have to decide if they are better off letting individuals decide (lower taxes) or having the government spend on their behalf (higher taxes).

Freedom from Government

This one is the other side of fiscal freedom and looks at the level of government spending rather than what governments collect from their citizens. Throughout the world, the average level of government spending is 31 percent of GDP; in the United States, it is approximately 21 percent.

Nations with the Highest Average Effective Tax Rates* for Business Capital Investment	
Congo	55.7
China	46.9
Argentina	44.3
Brazil	38.8
Germany	38.1
United States	38.0
Russia	37.6
Canada	36.6
Japan	32.2
France	32.1

Nations with the Lowest Average Effective Tax Rates* for Business Capital Investment	
Mexico	13.8
Singapore	11.5
Ghana	9.9
Ecuador	8.2
Ukraine	7.7
Hong Kong	6.1

Source: C.D. Howe Institute

*These rates include corporate tax rates, sales taxes, and any others related to capital investment.

Monetary Freedom

The monetary freedom measure can be thought of as an indicator of monetary policy; for example, it looks at things such as inflation and price controls that disrupt a currency's ability to function smoothly and reliably.

Investment Freedom

Here we have a measure of a country's openness to foreign investment. Not many countries have a high level of openness in this area, as fears abound of foreign control of domestic assets and visions of predatory investors taking off with the profits. The reality is that foreign investment, done well, brings new jobs and economic growth to the host country.

Financial Freedom

This measure looks at the openness of each nation's financial and banking systems. Though these must be sound and have clear controls, too much regulation stifles investment opportunities and hampers economic growth.

Property Rights

Property rights exist where individuals are free to do as they please, within the boundaries of law, with their own property—which includes themselves. The most prosperous countries all do a good job of protecting property rights. Unfortunately the majority of the world's countries still have a long way to go when it comes to this measure, and it shows in the frequent lack of economic development in nations with the potential to do much better.

Freedom from Corruption

Corruption exists where governments, individuals, and businesses are able to subvert legal restrictions or where effective legal frameworks don't exist. Not only is corruption expensive, it also creates a risky, uncertain climate that worries domestic and foreign investors and entrepreneurs alike.

Did You Know?

In a recent study aimed at measuring the cost of corrupt practices, the cost of traveling along two main roads in an Indonesian province were studied. On one, 396 stretch drivers would have to go through approximately 27 police checkpoints, military roadblocks, and weigh stations, and pay bribes exceeding the total pay of those working on the trucks.

Another study found that bribes are 8 percent of the cost of doing business in Uganda; yet another uncovered a 15 percent hike in the cost of hospital supplies in Buenos Aires due to bribes. There is a strong correlation between how corrupt a country is and average income; the more corrupt countries, such as Haiti and Russia, have much lower per capita GDPs than less corrupt countries such as the United States and Japan.

Source: The Economist, *12/9/06 and 5/03/07*

Labor Freedom

Though it is easy to understand the appeal of minimum wage laws, restrictions on the length of the work week, and protections from being fired, hamper economic development and growth. It is very difficult and expensive to fire workers in Argentina, for example, so companies are hesitant to hire new workers. Higher rates of unemployment go with rigid labor markets, which mean that efforts to protect existing jobs may decrease the amount and quality of new jobs.

Did You Know?

The worldwide average cost to fire an employee is equal to 54 weeks of salary. Employers keep that potential cost in mind as they consider new hires.

On the Trail of the Invisible Hand

With advances in theory and computing power, economists can now crunch far more economic data than in the past. This doesn't settle all disagreements, but it does allow many theories to be tested against empirical research that were largely accepted on faith (or the lack of it) in the past.

When Adam Smith wrote about the invisible hand, he wasn't referring to an outside force that pushed people along whether they liked it or not. What he meant, instead, was that a spontaneous order emerges from millions of people contributing their own choices to the mix each day, as though an invisible hand were guiding them to serve the interests of others. Individual decisions are coordinated by markets and changing prices. Changing prices match the nearly infinite array of goods and services some people produce and others purchase each week.

This is why the impact of economic freedom has been so hard to quantify. How do you measure the unseen? That being impossible, an alternative is to measure progress and prosperity. If indicators of economic freedom can be measured and compared across countries objectively, relationships between levels of economic freedom and income, inflation, and so on can be analyzed.

Come into the Light

The 157 countries examined for the *Index of Economic Freedom* are given scores in each of the 10 areas and then totaled to yield overall scores from 1 to 100. The higher the score, the freer the economy; the lower the score, the less free (or repressed) the economy. The following is a table showing the breakdown by category. As you can see, there are many more countries that are repressed and mostly unfree than countries that are free and mostly free.

Score	Category	Number of Countries
80–100	Free	7
70–79.9	Mostly free	23
60–69.9	Moderately free	48
50–59.9	Mostly unfree	59
0–49.9	Repressed	20

Source: Index of Economic Freedom, *2007*

In the seven economically free countries, citizens enjoy twice the average income of the countries just one level down, in the mostly free category. The contrast grows, too, for the top seven have average incomes that are five times the average of those in the repressed category. Not only that, but as you move up from repressed economies to free economies, rates of inflation and unemployment fall each step of the way.

The 20 freest countries, as a group, have remained pretty consistent throughout the years the *Index of Economic Freedom* has been around, though there is movement up and down. The differences in income, shown in the next section, are striking.

More Than Just Location

It is easy to assume that the countries with the highest levels of economic freedom and income must be those blessed with natural resources and peaceful existences, but that is not the case. The United States, of course, is a wealthy, economically free country blessed with abundant natural resources. But what about Hong Kong, where incomes are higher but natural resources are almost nil (for example, they have to import almost all their food, oil, and so on)? They show how economic freedom coupled with solid economic institutions spark wealth creation even in locations with scant resources that can be pulled from the ground. People in Hong Kong instead rely on human resources, which can generate more prosperity with the right institutions.

But what about past histories of warfare, deprivation, and colonization? Many of today's most successful economies were torn apart by strife in the past, be it war from within or exploitation from outside (Ireland, for example). Problems in a country's past do not seem to limit benefits from economic freedom. In fact, as seen in former Soviet Union countries such as Estonia, economic freedom administered well is the best salve for years of tough times.

Evidence for the Masses

When studying human behavior, it is very difficult to completely explain complicated phenomena using just one factor. The relationship between economic freedom and prosperity is no exception. As you will see in the following table, there is a strong relationship between the two, and economic freedom accounts for a large chunk of well-being. Culture, government, and luck, however, also play roles.

That said, the evidence is compelling. Look at the differences in income by quintile. The top quintile (20 percent of countries) is a long way from the bottom quintile.

Incomes of Countries According to Level of Economic Freedom

Quintile	Per Capita GDP in Dollars
First 20%	27,726
Second 20%	12,395
Third 20%	6,937
Fourth 20%	3,721
Fifth 20%	4,794

Source: World Development Indicators, World Bank, 2006

Now look at the differences in unemployment and inflation between the freest and least free economies (still in descending order). Freer economies not only do a better job of producing wealth, they generate more jobs and keep prices more stable through sound monetary policy. Sure, the free economies have some enormous disparities in individual incomes, but at the same time, the level of opportunity and stability is significantly better for the people of those nations.

Inflation and Unemployment Rates According to Level of Economic Freedom

Quintile	Unemployment Rate	Inflation Rate
First 20%	6.6	1.8
Second 20%	10.9	4.5
Third 20%	16.4	6.6
Fourth 20%	16.5	6.3
Fifth 20%	18.0	19.6

Source: World Development Indicators, World Bank, 2006

Let Freedom Ring?

Though the relationship between economic freedom and incomes the world over can now be clearly shown, it doesn't account for everything or put all compelling questions to rest. It is a great source of numeric data that measures much of what had not been measured before, but it does not put the yardstick along everything.

In Chapter 17, we talked about the environment, happiness, jobs, the overall quality of life, and their relationship to economics. As important as they are, much of what goes into them are either subjective or intangible factors. In other words, money isn't everything—but it does enable us to obtain much that makes life more livable.

The Least You Need to Know

- Economic freedom has as much to do with the right laws and institutions as it does the power for people to use resources as they wish.

- Nations whose governments have the tightest rein of their economies experience the lowest incomes.

- Corruption is much more expensive to society than just the amounts paid for bribes. Sound laws are key for economic development.

- A nation's wealth is not determined by resources that come from the ground but by the resources intrinsic to its people and processes.

Chapter 19

Talent's Tale

In This Chapter

- Assembling a talented workforce
- The competition from international talent
- Economic superstars and the wage gap
- Attracting new talent through immigration

You've probably heard the saying, "To the victor go the spoils." In today's global economic landscape, the new mantra should be "To the talented goes the cash." Despite all the worries that globalization will push down world salaries and living standards to the same subpar level, the more likely scenario is much different. Instead of an even tide everywhere, the most successful economies of the future will be those that best nurture, attract, and reward talent.

Battling for Brains

A case could be made that worrying about trade deficits, outsourcing, and the like is a waste of time in today's economy. Why? Because countries where talented workforces assemble and are allowed to do what they are good at will likely find that these issues are resolved by pure economic performance. In other words, the trade balance will follow from the "brain balance."

Did You Know? _____

In late summer 2004, a mysterious billboard appeared at a subway stop in Cambridge, Massachusetts. It challenged readers to solve a difficult math problem. Those enticed into meeting the challenge discovered that the correct answer led them to a website with another puzzle to solve. Eventually those who were successful at solving the problems found themselves at a site hosted by Google, the company of search engine fame, who had come up with the novel approach as a way of leading top-notch talent to them.

It's What's Inside That Really Counts

For something so important, there aren't any comprehensive definitions of what talent is when it comes to the global economy. Instead, it means a variety of things. For starters, there is the notion of talent being an innate ability, something a person is born with, such as an ear for music or a high aptitude for math. In this sense, talent is a resource similar to a vast oil reserve, a thing that has occurred naturally and needs to be discovered and tapped.

Talent is more than just something that occurs naturally. It can also be an aptitude or ability, within an organization or group, that can be developed and transformed. A talent or set of them can be learned and taught, too.

Talents can manifest themselves in many different ways, and at different times, too. Ray Kroc, who bought the original McDonald's restaurant and built a fast-food empire, was a 52-year-old selling milkshake machines when he came upon the opportunity. The ability to put customers at ease and have the right sense of humor at the right time can be a huge talent in one company, while number crunching or writing a concise analysis are the gold standards at another.

Ray Kroc was an entrepreneur. He saw potential in the original McDonald's that others didn't. Successful entrepreneurs create new products, firms, and sometimes whole industries through a mysterious combination of insight, focus, hard work, and good luck. And entrepreneurs are more likely to flourish in industries and countries that allow the most economic freedom to experiment with new ideas and enterprises.

Talent Is as Talent Does

Being so broad a concept, talent is easier to recognize through observation than to capture by definition. We know a talented software writer, entrepreneur, banker, or engineer when we see them in action and witness their unique achievements and contributions. The talented among us are usually born with a special ability or the capacity to develop one, but the education, training, encouragement, and rewards they receive are at least, or more, in enabling talents to flourish. In the right environment, talents blossom; in the wrong environment, they remain hidden, stunted, or wither away.

Did You Know? _____

An international poll of human resource managers, conducted by the Corporate Executive Board, found that the top priority for 75 percent of them was "attracting and retaining" talent. Of those, 62 percent expressed concern about impending shortages of talent. In a separate survey, the same organization heard from 4,000 hiring managers in more than 30 companies who claimed that the average quality of job candidates had dropped 10 percent since 2004 and that the average length of time to fill a vacant position had risen from 37 days to 51 days.

Source: The Economist

How Do You Account for What You Can't See?

One of the challenges posed by talent is that it is so hard to quantify its value. It is an intangible asset—for example, it doesn't have a price tag such as a piece of equipment and it is hard to predict how it will pay off in the future. On a balance sheet, there is no entry for "talent" as there is for cash, inventory, or buildings, yet in a world where an ever-increasing proportion of businesses are information-based, it is the very thing that determines the strength of the bottom line and whether companies thrive in the future.

Did You Know? _____

It has been estimated by Accenture, a management consultancy, that since 1980, the average value of intangible assets for firms listed on the Standard & Poor's 500 has risen from 20 percent to 70 percent.

Minds on the Move

In 2003, a survey done by the Society for Human Resource Management discovered that 83 percent of workers were "extremely" or "somewhat" likely to look for a new job when the economy recovered (which it did). What this indicates is that the loyalty of bygone days no longer exists. At one time, it wasn't unusual for college graduates to be hired at companies where they would spend their entire careers. Today, having witnessed what happens when companies downsize, get taken over, shut down, or move, workers are more likely to keep their eyes open for new opportunities, even when they are perfectly happy where they are.

Workers more willing to change jobs and locations come as an impending talent shortage is forecast by demographic trends. By 2025, the number of citizens between 15 and 64 will decline by 14 percent in Japan, 9 percent in Italy, and 7 percent in Germany. In China, a booming economy thirsty for qualified workers, the one-child-per-family policy is sure to have a significant impact on the available native-born talent pool in the years ahead. Even in the United States, with young people making up a higher proportion of the population, baby boomers entering their retirement years translate into huge losses of senior management talent.

A Meritocracy of the Mind

In our emerging global economy, talent matters much more than where you were born or what religion or ethnic group you belong to. This doesn't mean elites will cease to exist, just that the new elites will be talent elites and that recognition and rewards will be more closely tied to accomplishment.

Smart, Cheap, and Motivated

With geographical, technological, and cost barriers falling, the talented from across the globe are able to compete in ways that were not possible in the past. Somebody in Thailand who makes an exercise video, for example, can compete in the American market with a lot less sweat than it took even 10 years ago.

This competition can be scary to those in developed countries. Take India as an example. About 2.5 million Indians graduate from college every year, and in their ranks are some 400,000 engineers and 200,000 IT professionals. They are well educated, speak English, and are willing to work long hours for significantly less money than their counterparts in Germany, France, Britain, and the United States. Indian graduates, for example, work an average of 2,350 hours a year. In Germany, the average is 1,700 hours; in France, it's a little less.

It was one thing when Americans saw labor-intensive goods being made abroad, such as toys and textiles. Now, Americans are watching traditionally high-paying technology jobs go overseas. This is a source of fear for many in wealthy nations who worry that pay will fall and job opportunities will disappear. Some jobs have shifted to the developing world, and pay has fallen for some tasks that compete directly with low-cost labor overseas. But many workers and firms in the developed world have adapted by shifting to more sophisticated tasks that don't yet face direct overseas competition. And consulting firms, for example, can successfully bid for more work when they can split tasks between their overseas and domestic workforces.

When Demand Outruns Supply

The reason Americans don't have to worry about all the good jobs being taken is that there simply aren't enough people to fill them. As enormous as India's population is, only about 11 percent of its student-age population goes on to higher education. In India's high-tech sector, wages have been rising at approximately 16 percent a year, which indicates that competition for these workers and the limited supply of them drives wages up, just as it has in the western world. Turnover among high-tech Indian workers is about 40 percent a year. This also illustrates the effects of the competition for talent; workers leave for better opportunities.

Management talent is in even scarcer supply in big developing economies such as India and China, and their wages increase even faster. In fact, it is becoming more common for firms in these and other countries to bring in managerial talent from the West!

The following table shows percentages of employees from select countries who have been contacted by other organizations, a high-tech version of raiding the cookie jar:

Country	Percentage
India	56
China	51
Australia	28
Canada	25
United States	23
Britain	22

Source: Corporate Executive Board, Recruiting Roundtable, 2006

School Days Are Never Done

Not only do firms have to compete for talent, they also have to invest in its ongoing development. Just because a talent has been identified or already been tapped successfully, that doesn't mean it is a static resource to be dipped into until it's gone. In a fast-changing global economy, competition pushes firms to never stop building on the talents and skills at their disposal. This doesn't mean simply building on existing abilities, but also training workers to unearth and develop new talents.

To illustrate how involved and costly it is to find and train the right people, consider this example from Infosys (an Indian company): in March 2006, they went through 1.4 million applications; tested 164,000 of those who had applied; interviewed 48,700 of the applicants; then, finally, hired 21,000. As the previous table shows, more than half of these 21,000 new employees were soon contacted by competitors trying to lure them away. Now, after finding the right people and trying to keep them, Infosys has to invest in their ongoing training if they are to remain competitive. In 2006, their training budget rose from $100 million to $125 million.

Did You Know? _____

Finding talented workers and recruiting them has become surprisingly expensive. Accounting and consulting firm Deloitte has estimated that an average American company spends 50 times more to recruit a professional than the yearly cost to provide the same professional with ongoing training.

The phrase "Good help is hard to find" is truer today than ever before when it comes to talented workers—and it's much more expensive, too.

Countries and Clusters

Nations with large pools of talent have a few options. Their "best and brightest" can simply pick up and leave for greener pastures, which few nations like to see happen; or nations can create the conditions necessary for workers to stay and features that attract firms to set up shop within their borders.

General Electric has estimated that 60 percent of its growth in the next decade will occur in the developing world, a big increase from the 20 percent of the last decade. To fully understand emerging markets, it's necessary to have a presence in them. In addition, U.S. firms can draw from a large population of immigrants who have over the years worked their way up in leading American manufacturing, consulting, and investment firms. Who best to lead a major expansion in a developing country than a team that includes proven employees originally from that country?

As this trend continues, it won't be just the "dull" jobs that get done abroad, but an increasing amount of research and development, too. South Korea, Moscow, and Shanghai are examples of places where high-end work is done and opportunities for local talent abound.

For Whom the Bell Curves

In 1980, economist Sherwin Rosen introduced the idea of economic superstars: individuals or groups with unique goods and services who dramatically outperform the competition (as in a steep drop-off in revenue after the few, or only, at the top). Superstars offer something that is significantly better or more desirable than what can be found elsewhere, and it also must be available to a large market.

The most obvious examples of this phenomenon are found in sports and entertainment. Top athletes and actresses make millions a year while others in the same field, who may be very close in ability, make only a small fraction. Today, a similar thing is happening with the best talent. Not only do they earn more than others, but firms and nations with high concentrations of them can become economic superstars, places where the products are a cut above the competition and available to all who want them. Here great wealth will accrue; for those further down the pecking order, the distance between them and those at the top will increase.

 Did You Know? _____

The Wall Street Journal quoted Alan Eustace, a Google vice-president, as saying that a top engineer is worth "300 times or more than the average."

Making the Best Brighter

Global companies in competitive markets learn to economize in training those in their organization, and focus their resources where the greatest estimated payoffs are. This doesn't just happen at the top. Moving down the ladder but still within the talented rungs, the focus is also narrowing to the best there.

There is evidence to support this practice. As one example, the Corporate Executive Board estimates that the best computer programmers are more than 12 times as productive as an average programmer. Ask yourself, then, where you would concentrate a limited training budget.

 Did You Know? _____

Microsoft founder Bill Gates said, "If it weren't for 20 key people, Microsoft wouldn't be the company it is today."

Separate and Never Equal

The freest, most open labor markets exist in the United States. From CEOs to golfers, no other nation rewards those at the top of their games so richly. At the same time, there has long been concern that the gap between the wealthiest and the rest is growing. As it turns out, the percentage of national income going to the top 1 percent of earners doubled to 16 percent from 1980 to 2004. During the same period, the top .1 percent's share tripled to 7 percent.

The growing inequality in the United States is not unique. In developing countries, the differences are even more glaring. The talent elites cluster in wealthy areas, often in gated communities where the children go to private schools in preparation for attending top universities. It is not unusual for poverty, unemployment, poor health care, and minimal education to be the norm a short distance beyond the gates.

Did You Know?

Back in 1966, management guru Peter Drucker said, "Every knowledge worker in a modern organization is an 'executive' if, by virtue of his position or knowledge, he is responsible for a contribution that materially affects the capacity of the organization to perform and to obtain results."

In free countries, however, poverty, unemployment, and poor health are becoming less common. Regardless of how much the richest people earn, economic freedom disburses wealth through open economies. The "20 key people" at Microsoft helped make millionaires of thousands of less key employees as well as both astute and lucky investors. And these new millionaires in turn helped create good jobs with amazingly high incomes for developers, construction workers, landscapers, autoworkers, and untold thousands of everyday people working in restaurants, health clubs, and so on.

Thinking Ourselves Rich

For all we hear about immigration and the problems that accompany it, it is important to remember that educated workers are more mobile than untrained workers. And with talent shortages everywhere, any country that wants a vibrant economy can attract them from any corner, nook, or cranny of the globe. And thanks to the magic of exchange, when untrained workers are available to handle lawn mowing, weeding, and house cleaning, knowledge workers have more time and energy for creating value in their esoteric virtual worlds.

Hands On, Hands Off

Governments have become more proactive in using immigration laws to attract more talent. If you have a set of skills desired in Singapore or Ireland, the doors swing open a lot easier. And although more countries will do ever more to move heaven and Earth to bring in more of the talent elite, don't expect governments to recognize the value of those with less-developed talents.

Outsource This Way

Governments send mixed messages to high-skill workers overseas. Some agencies push to make it attractive for companies who employ talent to locate there. At the same time, some politicians and government agencies denounce both immigration and outsourcing. But even if the talent elite are working in your country for a foreign company, they increase wealth and spread know-how. Indeed, the talented are sought after and celebrated in whatever form they arrive, though less enthusiastically by those who compete directly for the same jobs.

The Least You Need to Know

◆ Talent is the world's most important resource, and there will never be enough of it to go around.

◆ The more barriers of cost, time, and politics fall, the more talent will migrate to the nations where it is best rewarded.

◆ Jobs, wealth, and a better quality of life will both follow and attract talent.

◆ In the future the split won't be between the industrialized and the developing worlds, but between the more talented and the less talented.

Glossary

ability to pay principle   Principle stating those with greater wealth should pay a higher percentage in taxes than those with less wealth.

absolute advantage   When a country can produce a good more cheaply than another country.

allocative efficiency   When resources have been divided and utilized to produce the array of goods and services most desired by consumers.

anti-dumping duty   A charge levied on a good that is judged to be selling below its cost to produce.

appreciate   When a currency's buying power goes up.

asset market approach   Using interest rates and expected movements in exchange rates to help decide which currencies to invest in.

balance of payments   The record of the monetary transactions between the residents of one country and the rest of the world.

barter   A type of trade where goods and services are traded for other goods and services without using money.

call option   Enables you to buy foreign currency at a set price.

comparative advantage   Exists when one country can produce a good or service at a lower opportunity cost than another.

complements   Goods that are used together.

consumption gains   Refers to the increased amounts of goods and services citizens of countries who specialize in areas of advantage and trade with other countries are able to consume.

coordination failure   When a positive outcome is not reached because those involved in the effort lack the means to jointly direct it efficiently.

crawling peg   A cross between a floating rate and a fixed rate.

credits   Payments residents of one country receive from another country in the balance of payment accounts.

currency   All coins and paper money.

currency swap   Takes place when banks convert one currency to another with the understanding that they will convert back at a particular time in the future.

current account   Keeps track of the goods and services sold by countries and those that are sold to them from other countries.

debits   Payments residents of one country make to another country in the balance of payments accounts.

developing countries   Countries with few capital goods, a lack of modern technology, poor health care, growing populations, high rates of illiteracy and unemployment, and agriculturally based economies.

domestic content requirement   Sets a minimum percentage of a good's value that must come from components made in the home country.

domestic subsidy   Provided to firms producing goods that compete with imports.

dumping   When less money is charged for a product sold abroad than is charged in the home country.

economy of scale   When a firm that increases their output of a product is able to lower their cost per unit at higher production levels.

entrepreneur   A person alert to opportunities others have not seen or acted on and who uses limited resources to produce new goods and services and bring them to the appropriate markets with the goal of earning profits.

equality-efficiency tradeoff   When an overall loss of economic efficiency follows
a reduction in income inequality.

exchange rate   Tells you how much of a particular currency must be sacrificed to get one unit of another currency.

export   A good or service that is produced in one country and sent to a foreign country for that country's consumers to purchase.

export subsidy   Subsidies given to firms producing goods for export to other countries.

factor endowment theory   States that differences between countries in comparative advantage can be explained by the variations in resources they have available and make use of.

Federal Reserve System   The central bank of the United States and is made up of
a Board of Governors and 12 Federal Reserve Banks spread around the country. Their job is to oversee the American banking system and manage the money with the goal of promoting full employment and steady, healthy economic growth while keeping inflation low.

fixed exchange rate   Rate tied to a major currency, such as the American dollar.

floating exchange rate   Rate determined by the free market forces of supply and demand.

forward transaction   Occurs when a specific amount of currency is contracted for but not paid for or received until a later date.

fractional reserve banking system   A system in which a specific percentage of checkable deposits has to be backed up with cash.

Gross Domestic Product (GDP)   The total market value of the goods and services produced during a specific year within the boundaries of a country. It includes production by both domestic- and foreign-owned concerns.

human capital   The productive value of education, training, experience, talent, health, and other resources possessed by workers.

import   A good or service produced in a foreign country and brought into a different country for purchase.

import quota   A limit on the amount of a good that can be imported into a country during a specific period of time.

infant industry argument   States that new industries should be protected until they achieve an economy of scale that enables them to compete on an equal basis with foreign competitors.

inferior goods   Those products that consumers purchase less of when their incomes rise and more of when their incomes fall.

interbank market   The process by which banks trade with each other.

investment   The portion of a country's current output that private firms use for future output.

joint venture   A partnership in which each firm contributes resources and shares in the risks and profits.

law of one price   States that identical products will cost the same no matter what nation they are purchased in.

macroeconomics   Is concerned with the economy as a whole and the major components of it, such as all household, business, and government sectors.

market   Any setting in which buyers and sellers come together to exchange their limited resources.

market economy   The decisions made by buyers and sellers to coordinate the allocation of resources.

market failure   When a market does not bring about the best overall allocation of resources.

market fundamentals   Consumer choice, government policy, productivity, inflation, and interest rates that influence supply and demand.

market system   All the markets involved in market economies.

microeconomics   Examines decisions made by individual units, such as individuals, households, and firms, and those made in markets for specific goods and services.

multinational company   Operates across national borders and may be owned and directed by individuals residing many miles away.

near-monies   Liquid financial assets that are not money but can easily be converted into currency.

nominal interest rates   Stated rates for financial assets.

non-tariff trade barrier (NTB)   Any measure besides a tariff enacted to restrict international trade.

normal goods   Products whose demand rises and falls with fluctuating incomes.

official exchange rate   A rate calculated by comparing the par values of two currencies.

opportunity cost   The value of the next best alternative, the one given up to make another choice.

option   Something purchased so that the buyer has the right to buy or sell financial instruments during a set time period in the future. There is no requirement that the right be exercised.

orderly marketing agreement   When countries participating in trade devise an agreement mandating who gets to participate in what segment of the market.

par value   In a fixed rate system, nations give their currency a par value, which is a statement of the money's value in terms of something else, such as gold or another currency.

persistent dumping   The continuous policy of selling a good for less abroad than is charged domestically.

predatory dumping The practice of temporarily lowering prices to drive a competitor out of business.

productivity The amount of a good or service that can be produced per hour of labor.

profit motive An individual's incentive to gain something of value that makes one better off.

purchasing power The amount of goods and services money can buy.

rational expectations theory States that individuals and firms adjust their decisions in response to changes in economic policy, which may result in the policy becoming ineffective.

real interest rates Rate calculated by starting with the nominal rate and subtracting inflation.

relative purchasing power parity States that changes in national price levels determine increases and decreases in exchange rates in the long run.

resource Anything that can be used to produce goods and services, including everything from oil and water to employees and computers.

scarce resources The finite amounts of land, labor, capital, and entrepreneurial ability that are never sufficient to satisfy the world's wants.

speculative attack When a weak currency faces strong selling pressure.

sporadic dumping Occurs when a competitor sells off excess inventory in another country for less than is charged at home.

spot transaction The purchase of foreign exchange for cash when the transaction is completed within two days.

store of value When money is set aside as an asset to be used in the future.

subsidy Financial assistance that the government provides to companies and specific sectors of the economy with the goal of promoting sales.

substitutes Goods that can be used in place of each other.

target exchange rate   Specific exchange rates a government decides upon and supports by entering exchange markets and buying or selling currency as needed.

technology transfer   When countries gain knowledge and skills from firms operating within their borders.

token money   Government-issued money, such as paper currency or coins, that has greater face value than intrinsic value.

tradeoff   When some or all of one economic alternative is given up to achieve another.

tragedy of the commons   Occurs when commonly owned natural resources are destroyed, overused, degraded, or neglected because no one has the authority or right to exclude users from overuse.

unintended consequence   Unforeseen outcome of a decision or course of action, usually used to describe negative results.

unit of account   Used to measure the value of money.

Internet Resources

United States Government Sites

Bureau of Economic Analysis, U.S. Department of Commerce www.bea.gov

Bureau of Labor Statistics, U.S. Department of Labor   www.bls.gov

Congressional Budget Office   www.cbo.gov

Federal Reserve System   www.federalreserve.gov

U.S. Census Bureau   www.census.gov

U.S. Department of Treasury   www.ustreas.gov

U.S. International Trade Commission   www.usitc.gov

Other Government and Economic Organization Sites

BREAD, Data from Developing Countries   http://chd.ucla.edu/dev_data

CountryReports   www.countryreports.org

EconStats   www.Econstats.com

European Union   http://europa.eu/index_en.htm

Global Financial Data   www.globalfindata.com

NationMaster   www.nationmaster.com

Organization for Economic Co-operation and Development   www.oecd.org

United Nations Common Database   http://unstats.un.org/unsd/cdb/cdb_help/cdb_quick_start.asp

The World Bank   www.worldbank.org

World Trade Organization   www.wto.org

Economic Association Sites

American Agricultural Economics Association   www.aaea.org

American Institute for Economic Research   www.aier.org

Arts, Sciences, and Engineering at Tufts University Global Development and Environment Institute   http://ase.tufts.edu/gdae/

Center for Economic Policy Analysis   www.newschool.edu/cepa/

Center for Global Development   www.cgdev.org

International Health Economics Association   www.healtheconomics.org

Appendix C

Further Reading in Economics

Books

Bhagwati, Jagdish. *In Defense of Globalization*. New York: Oxford University Press, 2005.

Easterly, William. *The Elusive Quest for Growth: Economists' Adventures and Misadventures in the Tropics*. Cambridge, MA: The MIT Press, 2002.

————. *The White Man's Burden: Why the West's Efforts to Aid the Rest Have Done So Much Ill and So Little Good*. New York: Penguin, 2006.

Friedman, Milton. *Capitalism and Freedom*. Chicago, IL: University of Chicago Press, 2002.

Krugman, Paul, and Maurice Obstfeld. *International Economics: Theory and Policy*. Indianapolis, IN: Addison-Wesley, 2005.

O'Rourke, P.J. *On the Wealth of Nations (Books That Changed the World)*. Atlantic Monthly Press, 2006.

Rivoli, Pietra. *The Travels of a T-Shirt in the Global Economy: An Economist Examines the Markets, Power, and Politics of World Trade.* Indianapolis, IN: Wiley, 2006.

Sachs, Jeffery. *The End of Poverty: Economic Possibilities for Our Time.* New York: Penguin, 2006.

Sen, Amartya. *Development as Freedom.* New York: Anchor, 2000.

Smith, Adam. *The Wealth of Nations.* New York: Modern Library, 2000.

Sowell, Thomas. *Basic Economics: A Common Sense Guide to the Economy.* Cambridge, MA: Perseus Books Group, 2007.

———. *Applied Economics: Thinking Beyond Stage One.* New York: Basic Books, 2003.

Stiglitz, Joseph. *Globalization and Its Discontents.* New York: W.W. Norton, 2003.

———. *Making Globalization Work.* New York: W.W. Norton, 2007.

Wolf, Martin. *Why Globalization Works.* New Haven, CT: Yale University Press, 2005.

Academic Journals

American Economic Review

American Economist

Asia-Pacific Development Journal

Contemporary Economic Policy

Developing Economies

Economic Affairs

Global Economic Review

International Economic Review

Journal of Development Economics

Magazines and Newspapers

Christian Science Monitor

Economist

Harvard International Review

International Business Statistics

International Trade Forum

Multinational Business Review

The Wall Street Journal

Index

D

J–K

L

Q-R

Great gifts for *any* occasion!

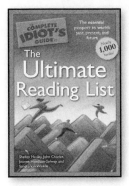

ISBN: 978-1-59257-645-6

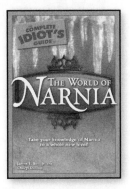

ISBN: 978-1-59257-617-3

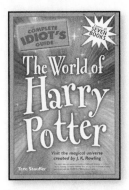

ISBN: 978-1-59257-599-2

ISBN: 978-1-59257-749-1

ISBN: 978-1-59257-557-2

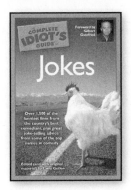

ISBN: 978-1-59257-538-1

ISBN: 978-1-59257-631-9

ISBN: 978-1-59257-715-6

ISBN: 978-1-59257-567-1